Beyond the Mountain

A memoir

Anita Vlismas, Ph.D.

little pink press™

This work depicts actual evens in the life of the author as truthfully as recollection permits and/or can be verified by research. Occasionally, dialogue consistent with the character or nature of the person speaking has been supplemented. All persons within are actual individuals; there are no composite characters.

DEDICATION

I dedicate this book to all who have done their best
to live well, indulge in enduring kindness, and
recognize each of us as part of "The All,"
past, present, and future.
Boundaries are illusory as we recognize we
are inexorably part of eternity.

ACKNOWLEDGMENTS

The longer I have lived, the more I realize the numbers of fellow humans and moments in the natural world I have embraced. Those who have shared their hearts, wisdom, hospitality and homes have been absorbed in that part of me that is eternal.

Family, friends, and acquaintances have unwittingly supported my writing of this book. They have heard only some of my stories. No individual has heard them all because I have protected myself from judgment or attempts to influence my decisions. The one exception is my editor, Bonnie Hearn Hill, whom I have trusted with understanding and accepting the values and continuum of my life. I am grateful to her and to Keryl Pesce, my publisher, for believing in this book.

During this year of writing, those who know my goal ask "How's the book? What are you writing about now?" I respond with a vague summary of which section of my life I am describing. I appreciate these cheerleaders, who include the doctors and nurses who are treating my peritoneal ovarian tubal cancer.

Sometimes those who have known me for decades help me with the details of family-centered memories. My siblings, Laureen Beckler, Richard Metz, and Daryl Metz have filled out some of my memory gaps. My best friend, Amanda Davis Hemley, knows me in depth because we have shared other adventures, love of the arts, families, and have generally explored our life choices. We have worked in the same studios and shared frustration with our creative abilities. Amanda is the one who reminds me to not worry about what others might think. "It's their problem if they don't understand your values and chosen lifestyles," she says.

Although I may seem to take them for granted, I want to emphasize how extremely thankful I am for my children, Aaron and Kurt Phinney, who have not yet disowned me. Their constant support and appreciation have been most significant in keeping me going, emotionally and physically. Diane, Aaron's wife, has provided home-cooked meals that remind me I still have a great appetite. Together, my children recurrently remind me my memory and energy exceeds that of many seniors they know, and this helps me keep writing and creating.

Today there are no friends or family who have known me since my birth. Those who initially said "You should write" are no longer in this life, but their belief in my capacity to capture and share what I have learned and experienced echoes in my mind each day.

Chapter One

We had arrived. Neil and I had everything we ever thought would make us happy—two sons, academic success, a home on the water. I was the perfect mother, the good woman, and still I wasn't happy. Maybe it was the weight of the halo I'd been wearing for most of my life. Maybe it was something else, a heavier weight I could not quite name.

The kids were all right now having had my ideal of a solid grounding in self-image and social values. We played in the snow, we baked cookies and pies and sometimes fried doughnuts. Kurt painted in oils while I made supper. Aaron tie-dyed his shirts and block printed peace signs on his bedroom curtains. Together we used the jigsaw to make wooden toys, and they knew how to use a vise and drill a hole. We went on rock-collecting expeditions. Pyrite crystals shined from our windowsills. I gave them matches to play with under my close supervision. They did not have to sneak as I did at age five. My parents had kept the mystery of matches away from me, so that in my own childhood, I had accidentally set the wash basket on fire. The flame under the hot water heater was an eternal mystery.

My parents never knew.

I absolutely loved playing with my children—for short periods of time. However, an undertow of resentment remained. I knew I had no real friends and no money for nursery school. Neil was having all the intellectual fun, and I remained home, often seated on the hardwood floor with my back literally against the wall. The children happily toddled over and around me. "Mommy. Mommy. Mommy." I was not always happy to play with them, but that was impossible for me to admit to anyone. The children never realized I really wanted to read my own books.

This cannot be all there is, I thought. I had followed the script. My home reflected the influence of *Good Housekeeping* magazine. Even Dr. Spocks's advice sometimes overrode my good sense of how to be a mother. Today, I know Spock was sometimes very wrong. In those days, loneliness prevailed. "Is it me?" I would ask myself. "Am I the problem?"

Neil and I were a team, and it was poignantly painful to realize his studies in economics and business were irrelevant to the philosopher he really was. The children attended school fulltime now, and Neil and I were able to explore our own ambitions.

Neil needed something more intellectually challenging than teaching high school. Respecting the super mom model of the sixties, we agreed that I would teach high school fulltime and college at night. He lovingly fed the children their evening meals, saw that they properly bathed, and put them to bed, often before I got home. When he graduated again, this time as a Ph.D., we hosted faculty parties that reflected the long gowns, stemware, and other trappings of the times. When someone would ask Neil, as they often did, "How did you get such a beautiful wife?" I held my breath. I cringed, not yet aware of how I appeared to others, knowing only that I would pay for the compli-

2

ment later. Although Neil was jealous, he had nothing to worry about with me. After all, my halo overruled premarital sex, and it most certainly overruled adultery.

Six years older than I, a Navy veteran, and a college student on the GI bill, he had been my best friend. We had dated for two years. I admired him for both working and attending school fulltime. The glue of our relationship was our passion for the great artists of the past, including Chekov, Tolstoy, Mahler, Wagner, Brancusi, Giacometti, Bonnard, and Matisse. We discussed philosophy and great literature constantly. Neil wrote poetry and could sing classical themes and variations with perfect pitch. An inch shorter than I, he frequently wore a white T-shirt with a pack of cigarettes rolled-up in his sleeve like Frank Sinatra in all those sailor movies. Furthermore, he could take over a dance floor—a talent I admired and never shared. On our second New Year's Eve, I kissed him, and that changed everything. I was passionate. He wanted sex, and so did I. I asked my mother if she would support our marrying. She said, "No. He just wants your money."

The fact that my family was far from rich meant nothing. She just didn't want me to marry him because he wasn't yet the doctor she had hoped for as her son-in-law. With no other options just before exams in 1957, Neil and I borrowed two hundred dollars from his parents and drove across the Indiana state line with my portable Royal typewriter. We wrote two term papers and studied enough to get A's on the philosophy exam despite the major distraction of breaking the sex taboo.

As a married couple, we were isolated from others. We had a small railroad apartment in the basement of a twelve-story apartment building. I could hear the rats scurrying along the beams between our ceiling and the main floor, and I could see the shoes and ankles of the people walking on the sidewalk through the ceiling-level windows. Plaster fell off the walls.

I decided to clean it up, so we painted everything white and gilded the walls. The unpredictable gilded patterns hid the defects. We also put in used Kelly-green carpeting and cut new linoleum for the tiny kitchen. Now, we were ready for company and the stimulating discussions we craved.

We picked four men from our classes and invited them over for coffee and conversation. Our topics ranged from politics to poetry, and those meetings added the social connection we were missing in our lives. Of course, I was the only woman at those gatherings, and I was the one who poured the coffee, but I had yet to question that role.

Soon we had that near perfect life — two sons, two dogs, two cars, two degrees. We used our station wagon during the many camping trips we could afford. Before seatbelts, we put a portable foam mattress in the back, and this allowed a place for the children to move and sleep. We carried a rock hammer and a skinny pocket manual to supplement my university studies in geology. I loved walking the creek beds and short rocky inclines looking for specimens. We kept few trophies because there was little room in the car. Being short and close to the ground, the children quickly saw and excitedly showed us creepy crawlies We rarely knew what they were beyond the broad categories of frogs, salamanders, bees, beetles, or spiders. More than a list to tick off places we had been, Yosemite, Mesa Verde, and Yellowstone National parks offered playgrounds that we mined.

Neil and I took turns driving, and we usually avoided restaurants. We visited Aunt Alice in Florida and my cousin who had married a Vietnamese woman he had met during the war. We boated and fished with the Ohio family and repeated trips to Cadillac Mountain near Bar Harbor, Maine, and Prince Edward Island, Canada.

An Oberlin professor offered the use of his empty

vacation cabin on Lake Pymatuning, Pennsylvania. We moved in for three weeks. Children and father, playing at the beach, gave me a few personal moments of uninterrupted bathroom time. Suddenly, I found myself sliding off the toilet. On the way down, ever the dignified mother, I grabbed a towel to cover my bare bum. My knees and head resting on the smelly, linoleum floor provided some stability, but I was frightened not knowing what was happening. I remembered I had extreme abdominal pain, and the commode was full. Sweat covered me, my blood pressure had dropped. I could not see or help myself. My horizontal body blocked the bathroom door. I feared my family would not be able to help me. I could hardly move. My trousers were still around my ankles. However, I managed to open the door a crack so they could save me. Later, the emergency room staff had no idea what had happened. Fortunately, I recovered within the hour.

With certainty, I now know that in life unexpected, uncontrollable vulnerability occurs frequently. As a child, living with my dad, I learned to "Toughen up. Don't belly ache." In one way, Doris Day's admonition, *"Que sera, sera"* is good advice. But for me, acceptance of what is, is simply the beginning. My next question that always follows is, "What's next?"

Sixteen years later, my family and I seated in our A-frame living room with its cathedral ceilings, I looked at Neil and our sons, Aaron and Kurt. I knew this was going to be tough. Our sons, almost teenagers, were gorgeous, trusting kids. How would I begin? How *could* I begin? On this beautiful spring day overlooking Centerport Harbor, in Long Island, I said, in what I felt was a calm voice, "I have something to tell you. We need to make a change."

"Why?" someone asked, or maybe no one did. Maybe I was just asking myself.

"I need space. I need to live closer to the campus. I'm

5

losing more than two hours a day just traveling."

All three were shocked. I spotted tears in the boys' eyes.

"I'm not deserting you," I told them. "I'm just taking a leave of absence. I need to concentrate on school, but I can be here to cook, to do laundry, to help you with your studies."

Everyone nodded. Neil appeared stunned, catatonic. Here I was, this cherished icon of love and motherhood, and I was going to abandon him for the university. Or so he thought.

In my second graduate program, I still felt like the dummy in my classes, just as I had in grammar and high school. I never got that confidence that I could do things other children could not. After marrying at the end of our sophomore year and coming back to take finals, I believed my job as a newly married wife in 1957 was to support my husband. Wives were to wear crinoline aprons when company came and put the man and children first. I worked twenty hours a week waitressing, and Neil worked full time in production control. Still, with my scholarship and his VA funding, along with the earnings we could bring in, we made it through school in a timely manner without debt. The script for young married women read like this. Be married, have children, and continue to be the little woman behind the man. I helped him get his degree and took his lecture notes when exhaustion prevented him from attending class. After college, when I was pregnant, I was a social worker, taking a bus to the workplace, and occasionally getting off the bus to get sick at the curb of the street.

There was no need for me to earn an advanced degree, and besides I wasn't that smart. Of course, my husband was smarter. I helped him get his master's degree, and he left the world of business and began moving into the world of teaching, which is where I felt he belonged. I continued working at every opportunity, worked two jobs, and then helped him get his Ph.D. Finally, I realized *I'm as smart as he is. I deserve the same recognition. It's my turn.*

I earned a master's degree, so I could teach in the community college. That was okay, but then I asked, "Is this all there is?" I had visions of myself conquering the world, and so I applied to the Stony Brook Department of Psychology for a Ph.D. In my first year of graduate school, I had lunch with the department chair, and we discussed what I was interested in. He said he was doing research on human sexuality, and I became involved in that research, attending seminars, writing erotic stimuli, short stories for the research projects, and finally actually measuring the degree of arousal using plethysmographs. Even though I didn't have physical experience, I had attained an incredible amount of theoretical experience.

Still, I couldn't ignore the increasing awareness that something was deeply wrong with my marriage. The more I learned about human behavior, the harder I tried to justify Neil's behavior. Sure, he drank. Sure, he went to see his mother every day for lunch and returned depressed. But I had always been there for him. The only therapy I knew was walking, and we did that whenever he came home from his mother's or the university, demoralized. His kisses felt limp, sad, without arousal. They reflected his own childhood abuse and feelings of inadequacy.

Our seminars in graduate school included interviews with people of all sexual varieties and experience. We were designing research to follow Masters' and Johnson's ground-breaking work. *Sex Without Guilt,* by Albert Ellis opened my eyes and imagination to other options.

Enter Gene. Eleven years older than my classmates, I was a mature, beautiful woman, and he was the super stud. Tall, lean, strong, and extremely confident, he was flagrant about his sexuality. I was smitten. He was in graduate school because he didn't want to go to Vietnam (Viet Nam back then), and I was there because with my $600-a-month stipend and future internships, I could afford the promise it offered me—to get to the top without jeopardizing my family's lifestyle. At that time, the top to me translated to a Ph.D., a doctorate. I truly wanted very much to learn what makes people behave in the ways they do. More than anything, I wanted to be of service, to help others live fully.

Fourteen of us had been gleaned from the thousands who applied. When I invited the class to a barbecue at my house on the water, they met Neil and the kids. Gene was part of that group. He and I frequently went out for coffee, and he shared tales of his conquests with me. One evening, as we waited for his train, I was aware of the absolute incongruity of my situation. Looking at four glass half-gallon jugs of whole milk positioned under Gene's long legs on the passenger side I asked, "Gene, have you ever had sex with an older woman?"

"No." He glanced over at me. "But I'd never pass up a fuck if one was offered."

That first time in bed with him lasted four hours. I had never had sex anywhere like that. After two weeks, I knew I couldn't continue cheating. I had to be with him.

Surely, I could work it out. Surely, I could figure out a way to be everything for everyone. As I sat by myself on the ugly green leatherette couch in the faculty room, I listed on my legal pad the pros and cons of staying married while the other students jabbered around me. What would I lose? Whom would I hurt? My kids were past the formative years. They would be fine. Besides, I'd be back every week and see that the laundry was done and meals for the week cooked and frozen. Putting everything on paper had helped me conclude that I could leave. An unrestrictive, uncensored life was possible for me.

The previous year, I had been a supervisor of student

teachers as they qualified for their licenses. One of my students had a cottage on nearby Crab Meadow Beach. I asked if I could rent it, and she said, "Of course." That was my intention. I never wanted to abandon the family, and this was only three miles away.

To Gene, I said, "I can move in with a group of girls, or I can move in with you."

"Yeah," he said, laid back as usual, Mr. Cool all the way. "Let's give it a try."

So, we gave it a try, and the cost was my marriage.

***

The story starts before this ending, of course. If I could look back and single out the moment my marriage was doomed, I couldn't. It was probably a series of moments in my life and Neil's long before we met.

To say I strove for perfection in my childhood is probably an understatement. The halo was firmly affixed before I met Neil. "Major Work, Major Jerk." That's what the gifted kids were called in elementary school, and painfully, I was one of them. My mother had decided I should be enrolled early, so at the age of four, I was evaluated by the Cleveland Public City Schools' psychologist, Dr. Lucky, for early admission to kindergarten. Talk about pressure from parents. Although far from what it is today in the world of helicopter parents who teach their young children to be concerned about grades because if they do poorly, they will not get into college, even then, the pressure on me outwardly appeared supportive, but it was heavy.

I did well in that first evaluation and allowed early admission, not knowing I was being put into an experimental program. So, I was my very own first clinical subject.

This Major Work program was led by a Dr. de Sauzee in the Western Reserve University Psychology Department. One of his locations was in Cleveland, another was in one of the New York boroughs, and the third was somewhere in

California. His program involved twenty-five to thirty children whom he followed from first grade until age thirty. This longitudinal study was funded to enrich these children's programs beyond the normal curriculum. Would it make a difference?

I was painfully aware of what my ranking was, having "accidentally" read the teacher's list of our IQs, and I felt I was the dummy in the classroom. Today, I am aware of the six-point variation on any IQ testing, and the reality that an IQ test measures academic skills, not overall intelligence. If the experiment had an arbitrary cutoff of 135, I could and probably made it by the scraping of my knees. It gave me the position in this group to always be at the bottom of the scoring. If there were A pluses to be earned, even in college, I always got the A or the A minus. I had little confidence in my intellect because I always compared myself to these so-called geniuses.

Each morning in elementary school began with a three-minute morning talk by one of our classmates. In addition to this sure bet method to counter public speaking phobia, the most common of all phobias, each semester we each submitted a special interest report of ten to twenty pages. I begged for and got a typewriter when I was in the fifth grade. If the number of pages mattered to the teacher, I gave it to her. I typed all reports double-spaced between the lines and between the words.

Because of our enriched curriculum, we were encouraged to research our own interests. I loved horses and was interested in the horses of the Cleveland Police Department. I went to the police barn and actually counted them, walked up and down the aisles, checking their diet and maintenance routines. For other reports, I asked various questions of myself such as, "Why do leaves fall?" "Why are people afraid of spiders?" Another one was, "Why is dirt made up of so many colors?" Now, this was elementary school, and my parents were traveling whenever there was a union layoff or strike. I always took samples in my brother's baby food jars and had the most colorful dirt collection contrasting with the gray earth of Ohio. This was way before people were making sand designs in fishbowls. I cannot remember if I made a report on that collection, but I sure enjoyed creating it, and it was probably the antecedent to my geology and geography science courses at the university. I avoided physics and chemistry because in high school I had to get a tutor for those subjects, and, although I did ace them, they were definitely challenging to me.

How I became intrigued with spiders I will never know, but I had the neighbor kids always looking for new additions to my collection. Again, those baby food jars came in very handy.

My hobbies and interests were not like those of the other girls. Practicing the piano was not one of them. I can remember crying as I sat on the scarred round top stool that would elevate as I turned the seat. It was a beautiful wood —probably mahogany—that arrived with the upright which was highly polished, properly tuned, and waiting for a less-than-reluctant prodigy. When Grandpa and Grandma came for Sunday dinner or when I had one of the few recitals at my piano teacher Ida Engle's house, I wasn't the most accomplished student, but my mother compensated by sending me to perform in velvet dresses, my hair in Shirley Temple rag curls. I did love music, and I always polished my saddle shoes to the WDOK classical music station.

I played the piano from age four to eleven. Each lesson was two dollars, and I walked two miles each way to Mrs. Engle's house. When I went to the junior high school, the school's music teacher, Mr. Whitney, really needed someone for the French horn. He gave me an evaluation called the *Seashore Test of Musical Ability*, (named after the psychologist who created it), and said I had the capacity to play this difficult instrument. The only catch was the horn cost six hundred dollars. Because my family could not afford that investment, the school paid for it, and my mother bought the mouthpiece, which at seven dollars, was much more affordable.

I loved the sounds of the orchestra and the pomp. Most of all, I loved the social aspect of playing the horn. When we organized as a band, we played at football games. As an orchestra, we gave concerts and participated in competitions. Unlike the piano, which for me was isolating, the horn gave me a reason to get to know other kids. Along with the social benefits, the horn made me physically stronger, and it also increased the determination aspect my personality. I was not stubborn but definitely determined. For me, this meant taking a goal and going for it, come hell or high water. It was just another mountain to intentionally climb.

Finally, my friends with disabilities provided an avenue for me to show kindness. I felt for them. One of the kids had webbed fingers, another stuttered, and the third, although extremely artistic, chronically dripped green snot. No one would work with him on joint projects, so I did. At that time in my life, I was Mother Teresa, without nursing skills. "Spread love everywhere you go. Let no one come to you without leaving happier."

I was gangly, still wearing undershirts until the ninth grade. How I wished I could play the flute, which was so tiny and so girly. Instead, here I was, lugging this big horn case onto the bus, actually two city buses, to be exact—which would take me to school. On the days I took the horn home with me to practice, I carried it, along with all my books. I can remember many times when it was icy, seriously cold, and snowing, and there I was, gripping the handle of the horn case, red knuckles documenting another cold winter trip to school. Because of that early musical training, I have always had great passion for horn solos, and quintets. Many famous symphonic compositions have great horn passages, wonderful opportunities to show off remarkable tones and rhythms independent of the other instruments. They are the moments in music that take me flying through the clouds.

I found in the simplest of art projects, I wanted to be copying what my neighbor was doing at the same table, never giving myself credit that I had learned two musical instruments, was competing in city- and state-wide competitions, and returned home with awards, but never first-place ones.

Besides special classes with an art teacher a couple of times a week, we had lessons in French with a teacher who was born in France, who spoke faster than we could, and who always focused on our accents. In college, I was reading Voltaire, Balzac, and Baudelaire in French, and also translating some Russian. I already had learned German at home. I swear my ear was never good, but somehow, I survived the courses and got my A's and sometimes B's.

In ninth grade, I wanted to win the French medal. It was another mountain for me, another goal. By that time, our original class had been assigned to different schools, and only four of the children with whom I had attended elementary school accompanied me to junior high. I had been studying French since elementary school, and I wanted that piece of paper that said I was better than or as good as that peer group that had come into the school with me. Again, I saw myself as not as skilled nor as beautiful and powerful as my competition. I was rigorously competing with Carole, a cheerleader, and I hired a tutor to increase my competency in French. Carole got the medal, but I tried. The guy she loved invited me to his prom. He was in our group, and when he chose a college different from hers, she followed him the next semester. Eventually he married Carole and became an engineer. The last time I saw them, she was working as an aerobics teacher in a local health club and had painted fingernails.

Sports weren't a particular strength of mine, but I loved swimming. By eleventh grade, I was a certified Red Cross swimming instructor and lifeguard. That summer, I was hired to be the head lifeguard and head swimming teacher at a small summer camp for younger children. This was Ohio, and all the instructors wore their sweatshirts with their bright red crosses as we taught shivering children. Not one child learned how to swim that summer. It was just too cold. However, I did enjoy the swimming and racing with other classmates, and when I got the opportunity to work at a Girl Scout Camp, I was teaching canoeing, showing my charges how to tip their own canoes, empty them of water, and right them again.

One achievement that clearly separated me from my classmates was a well-used 1952 Oldsmobile I bought two weeks after turning sixteen. The money for the car came from my savings from working with my dad and the sixteen dollars I earned each time I brought home a consecutive straight A report card. My dad paid for the insurance and gas. During my last year in high school, I was the only one who could drive my friends to the football games in my own car.

Another source of great satisfaction was helping customers of a wallpaper and paint outlet store. I would help them decide on colors, coordinating interior and exterior paint and then the more complicated job of selecting multi-colored wallpapers. One high-achieving couple, both lawyers, jumped at my suggestion that we could have damask patterned, flocked, silk wallpaper made to order for their dining room. Later, they came back to the store and gave me a handmade fused glass dish to underscore their appreciation. It was signed by Edris Eckhardt (1905-1998), who was a master teacher of sculpted glass for thirty years at the Cleveland Institute of Art. I often saw her exhibits. Today her work is in museums around the world, and the gift continues to remind me of her contributions in the field of glass sculpture.

I was not the class valedictorian, but as usual, close to the top. I knew in the nation, I tested out in the top 2 percent. At school, I was not number one, and I wanted to be. The idea of being the dummy of the class initially discouraged my efforts long after graduation. Every year, I would receive a questionnaire from Dr. de Sauzee, and one of the important questions was, "What is your current profession?"

I was either homemaking or going to school, but never achieving an acceptable professional status. Having been exposed to great art and music, I wanted it all. Now, with Neil's new earnings, we could afford an impressive Webcor phonograph and season tickets to the Cleveland Symphony Orchestra, George Szell conducting. However, I knew that access to original paintings and sculptures or furniture designed by Hermann Miller or Eero Saarinen or a home designed by Phillip Johnson were far beyond Neil's earnings as a public-school teacher. Whatever the symbols of a fine arts education I foolishly coveted, I would have to earn them myself. It would not be fair of me to expect my partner to just get out there and make money.

As a result, I decided to create my own original art. I attended classes at the Karamu Settlement House, which is still located in a rough neighborhood of east Cleveland. Initially developed in the 1920s to promote interracial theatre, the center expanded to include integrated classes for young and old in other arts. My sixty-year-old teacher, whose history included serving as a bodyguard for Trotsky in Mexico, a friendship with Diego Rivera, and sculpting the stone pediment of a Texas government building, became an influential friend. He and his wife celebrated his birthday and five New Year Eve dinners at our home. He taught me how to mix different clays in fifty-gallon garbage cans, the results of different kinds of firing and temperatures, and the importance of working from a live model. His voice has echoed throughout my life. "If you don't like a situation, change it. If you cannot see the model, move. Do not passively accept what is."

Because of his advice, I began to look at small barriers —juggling budgets, grading English papers on weekends. After that, I would always ask myself, "What's my problem? What can I do to change it?" Years later, I would use that same philosophy in assessing my own marriage.

Leaving my artist friend in Cleveland, I moved to Long Island, where my husband taught at the university, and I entered a doctoral program in psychology. I was motivated by the possibility of increased personal status and income, and of course wanting to make a difference. However, I again felt like the dummy. Here I was thirty-one-years old and here were these younger twenty-one-year-old students. Already published, they seemed like genius whiz kids. Later, I realized I had accrued wisdom and common sense, which became invaluable in our collective analyses of research designs and outcome evaluations. Experience in marriage, parenting, and working provided me with a different kind of confidence and point of view about "science." The Major Work Program ended the year I graduated from university the third time. There were no more follow-ups. I still wonder if my personal data would have changed anything. Were there any woman at the age of thirty-one who would yet become doctors or academic achievers or engineers because of that longitudinal study? How can you measure the effects of encouragement to follow aberrant interests? Think dirt, horses, spiders, leaves, elephants, coffee.

My fellow grad students took me under their wings, knowing how different I was. They encouraged me to be less of a nerd. "Why don't you undo that bun and wear your hair long? You can be hip."

I asked, "What's hip?" Even that had to be explained. They told me to buy jeans, show a bit of curve. So, the older woman and the younger, gifted generation exchanged strengths. I was learning that seeking the highest levels of "achievement" is not necessarily the best way to create an empathic, loving citizenry. I was gradually detaching from the old rules and re-identifying myself.

ANITA VLISMAS

Chapter Two

I was the eldest of four children in our family. My brother Richard was four years younger than I, my sister Laureen was six years younger, and Daryl was sixteen years younger. When I was supposed to be babysitting Daryl, I drove across town to hang out with a friend who was a teen mother. Daryl was carefully wrapped in his bunting on the backseat. We did not have car seats nor seat belts in those years. This probably wasn't a good idea, considering that I was a new, untested driver—but then, nobody knew.

When I left to drive home with my make-believe child again carefully placed on the backseat, my test arrived. In the alley behind my friend's house a heavy rain had created mud, lots of it. My wheels immediately began to spin and spin, no matter which gear I used. My heart raced. I could be in big trouble with this situation. I had taken my brother out of the house to visit a fallen woman without permission. No matter which direction I turned the wheels or which gear I chose, I could not get enough traction to move the car. The mud felt like two feet of unplowed snow. The weather was brisk. I had no money for a tow truck. I could not walk home. I did not want my parents to know what I had done. I had an infant in my care, and he would be hungry soon. The situation was not good. As I sat there weighing my options, out of the blue, I remembered that the car had floor mats. That was my answer. With the traction of the folded mats stuffed between the wheels and the mud, I gathered power. Like Wonder Woman, I felt as if I were flying although in reality I was just slowly advancing to avoid any other problems. My secret was safe.

My dad should have had only sons, but they would probably have been killed because of his intolerance for screw-ups. His relationship with my brothers, both of them over six feet, sometimes escalated to violence. But I usually avoided his targeting me. I never hated him. I just learned to do what he wanted and kept clandestine thoughts to myself.

My father was an equal-opportunity parent, and he expected me to do any job a man could, including backing a trailer down a steep hill the first year I was driving. He also expected me to anticipate what his needs were, much like a surgeon's assistant—and I had better anticipate correctly. Side by side, we worked, and I handed him tools before he asked for them. I sold Christmas trees on a vacant lot. I helped him paint our house. When I came home for a lunch break one day, running down the hill, my hands in my pockets, I fell, and thus arrived with a scraped nose. My father's response? "Never run with your hands in your pockets."

Once, he walked in to see milk I had spilled onto the kitchen floor and demanded, "What happened?"

"I had an accident," I replied, my voice close to inaudible.

His gruff reply? "There are no such things as accidents."

In his world of expectation, there was no such thing as

a mistake either. You could have controlled that, could have anticipated, could have planned. That's how I learned sequencing. I'm great at anticipating "cause and effect." "What's the cause?" "What are the gains?" "What is the down side of this event?" I also learned that we have only this moment. The past is done, having left its effects. *Do not become mired in the past. Do not ever tell anyone about that mud.*

Daydreaming about the future is different from sequencing. If I'm sequencing, I'm laying out a strategy. I'm aware of the realities of that decision, the way I did when I sat on that awful crackled leatherette green sofa and figured out whether to leave Neil. If you're living in the future, you're creating a fantasy world, a dream. As you read this book, you will see that I did my share of strategic planning. There was little time for dreaming.

Besides a head for creating income, my father was also a gifted tool and die maker and graduated in the top four in his class of one thousand from West Technical High School. During those high school days, he also had a paper route and delivered papers printed in six languages. He spoke only German until he was six years old and then learned English in the first grade.

At the peak of the depression, he always found work. Delivering orders for the May Company, he fell off the back of the truck and hit his head. His mother—my Grandma—said he was never the same, thus excusing his increasingly explosive anger. When that job ended, he rode the flatbed railroad cars to California, always looking for work.

When he returned to Ohio, he married Mom, and I was born a year later. They lived in my dad's parents' attic to save money, and both worked. Grandpa, who was twenty-five years older than Grandma, a retired bicycle maker, played the horses. Every day, he read the racing form. He babysat me when I was an infant, and when I cried, he gave me a strip of raw bacon as a pacifier. When my mother came in and saw me sucking on raw bacon, she screamed, and I survived without trichinosis.

When I was about one, my father came home drunk only once. Mom having lived with and run away from a drunken stepfather at age fourteen, said, "No way." She immediately vacated their home, taking me with her. She found work and moved in with Mrs. Gaebler, a social worker, her engineer husband, and their three kids. She was their nanny/homemaker. After a couple of months, Dad was allowed to visit, and they eventually worked it out. Mom remained friends with Mrs. Gaebler, and I stayed in touch with the children.

When I was four, Grandpa would dress me in my navy-blue velvet dress and take me to the track. We spent a lot of time in the paddocks, talking to the jockeys and evaluating the horses. He knew all the trainers and the jockeys.

That same year, my parents bought a house two miles from the Cleveland Zoo for four thousand dollars. It sat on a forty-foot-wide lot, on a red-brick street and had a full front porch. My dad put in a concrete driveway, a brick garage, and a scalloped picket fence. He later made a huge swing set with travel bars he crafted from steel. My first bicycle was another of his creations. It had twenty-four-inch wheels and was painted red. I don't know where he got the metal and believe he probably took it from the places he worked. When he taught me how to ride, he took me to the baseball field within the zoo so that when I fell, I would have a soft place to land.

Everyone on the street leaned their garbage cans against their garages, which was not only smelly, but attracted flies. Nobody had sunken cans. My mom solved the aesthetics of our garbage by having Dad install our two cans. When we bought the house, it had an ice box, and the ice man driving a horse and wagon, delivered the ice in fifty-pound blocks. Neighbors salvaged the manure for their roses. We moved up in the world when we bought a refrigerator.

Inside the house, Mom, in those days, an interior décorator, used all her skills to make our house the most beautiful one on the street. We had maroon wall-to-wall wool carpeting. In the kitchen, we had five feet of plastic tile on the walls, making them washable. She had Dad build a pantry in the kitchen and an extra toilet in the basement. Made of canvas, Waltex was an expensive wall covering of the day as was grass cloth. We had both throughout the house. Brushing against the grass cloth, I always could smell the islands I imagined as its sources.

I learned at that early age you can make or repair almost anything if you have the right tools. I was taught how to sole my shoes using a last and modify the layout of my shared bedroom so I could have a built-in desk. I sewed my Vogue evening gowns, always wanting to show a bit of décolletage with little to work with. Mother sewed many of my clothes, creating skirts with matching boleros from the used feed sacks my aunt gave us from her farm.

As a family, we also learned to live with omnipresent, underlying tension. Dad's unpredictability and imminent threat were facts of life, and I still feel the pain and shock when he so forcefully punched my brother that his neck jerked.

"Not on the face," Mom screamed. "Not on the face."

This brother was the one who got it the most because he never did learn to keep his mouth shut. The younger brother avoided him as much as possible. For a time, he too grew up with images of violent retaliation for our father's mistreatment.

We never knew—I never knew—when our dad would explode. Take, for instance, Sunday dinners at our house with Grandma and Grandpa. After church, we had chicken and Mogen David wine. Even we children were allowed a tiny amount, which might not have been such a bad idea considering the uncertainty of such occasions. Setting the table with the best damask tablecloth and napkins, china, and stemware, I could not predict any problems. However underlying the whole afternoon was a wariness that in our home, when Dad was around, his yelling and rage could change the entire agenda. If something wasn't right for him, he might yank that beautiful damask tablecloth from under the treasures of a working-class family. His tirades were scary. We never knew when all the plates, napkins, sterling, water and wine glasses, and crystal salt and pepper shakers would go flying.

All of us sat there in shock, not knowing what happened or how to proceed. Mom, however, covered for Dad as she always did, saying, "We will just clean this up." And she took another Librium. Some things she could not clean up.

Although my mother was the great fixer, I also noticed that she was cold to my father. She had fibroid breast cysts, and perhaps neither of them understood that was why his touching her breasts caused pain. All I saw was when he tried to hug her at the kitchen sink, she pulled away. I felt bad for him. Nevertheless, their relationship and our uncertain household motivated me to find a safe haven away from home. I found it at the Cleveland Public Library. The library back then was like the internet now, only warmer, more welcoming, and more anonymous. No one traced my search history or tried to scam me, and the only trolls were in fairytales. I could look at, touch, smell these books. I initially loaded up on all the Grimm fairy tales, and later, other more adult topics related to my special interests, international spying, strong women, marriage, and of course, sex. I think I was always invited to the pajama parties because I was the girl who knew all about female anatomy and what did what.

I'm surprised I'm not more anxious than I am, but I do admit I was a nail biter in the classroom and sometimes even today. It's been twenty years since I gained some control over the habit, but I've treated a lot of youngsters and have great empathy for them. One of my guidelines is, "If you are going to bite your fingernails, really enjoy it!" Works for me, and of course, it eventually hurts enough that we nail biters usually stop. You never see someone who has bitten off his or her finger although there are other kinds of personal maiming. Of these, I have no experience.

Still, having lived with the imminent explosiveness and physical pain generated by my father toward what often appeared as random targets, I became conditioned in a strangely positive way. Events can occur without expectation or intent. We learn to avoid pain by not touching a hot stove. I was conditioned to not foster my father's anger. But there was no sense worrying about when it was going to happen because that was something totally out of my control. This conditioning followed me through life. Worry is a waste of time and life juice. Identify a problem, and then do something about it, if possible.

While writing this book, I awakened from a dream. A large stranger was approaching my house situated in an isolated field. He tossed a long-barreled gun back and forth between his hands. The situation immediately felt foreboding. I awakened quickly and considered survival actions including use of my own gun. Then I systematically considered the many other options before me. Never did I feel terror or anxiety. Because of my history, I simply put all my thinking into possible solutions to the problem before me.

If the problem at hand is beyond my control, competence, financial capacity, or physical strength, I find it helpful to focus on what I can do to enjoy the day and thrive. Perhaps the unexpected environment I grew up with—that knowledge that anything goes, and anything can happen—prepared me for what I might otherwise have viewed as frightening situations. For example, when I was about four, I took the streetcar the two miles to church alone. My mother, on bed rest because of her fragile pregnancy with my younger brother, could not accompany me, and I really wanted to go. The streetcars built with cane seats and a little coal stove in the middle car, did not threaten me. I rode them to church alone and later, to the downtown library without fear. I just got on, paid my dime, and took a seat. I rode without trepidation. It was easier than the daily six-block walk to elementary school.

My mother was a confusing role model, and I internalized her many strengths. I had seen her laying sewer tiles, standing on roofs to repair a loose gutter, in addition to removing wallpaper and painting houses. On the other hand, she often counseled contractors as they built new developments and needed enticing model homes, inside and out. As a beautiful woman she appeared at construction sites wearing an eye-catching chartreuse caped coat with three-quarter length gloves and a patent leather hat with matching shoes. Upon arriving, she often called out "There's a woman on the job. No swearing." She could not control Dad's language or temper, but these workmen minded her.

Mother often relied on me to get the evening meals started at least twice a week. These were either meatloaf with a cottage cheese/head lettuce salad or chili con carne made with two cans of beans, a quart jar of preserved tomatoes and a pound of hamburger, fried with onions.

We children avoided our dad, anticipating his schedule and making a point of being elsewhere whenever possible. He always seemed to be involved with two or three daytime businesses, as he consistently worked the night shift, from 11 p.m. to 7 a.m, at the Ford Motor or Chrysler stamping plants. Both parents were definitely motivated to build a better life, challenging us to learn a new word a day, and to use library research to solve arguments. How easy it would have been if we had computers in the 1940s.

Dad's daytime businesses included buying and selling real estate, the trimming, cutting and removing of tree stumps, door to door sales of "new inventions," UPS truck deliveries, a painting and decorating business, which often relied on my mother's skills, and a machine shop that built parts for the federal government. Whenever possible, he engaged all the family in his world of work. Of course, education was always first on his agenda, but there were many opportunities to earn money, including door-to-door sales, sorting and delivering packages in the UPS truck, or working the lathe or grinding "tits and burrs" in the machine shop. He also taught me to send statements for his accounts receivable or pay his companies' bills. I never forgot to deduct his 10 percent discounts for early payments.

My underlying takeaway from this non-discriminatory parenting by both parents was if you want to do something, consider the sequence necessary to make it happen and the gains versus the risks.

Later, as a young mother, when my children and I wanted to sail our thirteen-foot Sunfish sailboat across the harbor, I insisted on safety precautions. We wore life jackets. We could swim. If the wind strengthened, and our boat unexpectedly flipped so that the sail lay flat in the water, we had already practiced what we might do when we were close to our home shore. My two preadolescent boys and I enjoyed the challenge and always made it to shore by righting our boat and sailing, or simply swimming it to shore. I didn't let the fear of what could happen stop us from our adventures.

This feeling, almost a philosophy, became even stronger in the future when I dealt with real long-distance sailing and real hurricanes.

In childhood, I had been successfully conditioned for life's reality. What is, is, and that's what I'm left with. It is the reality of any single moment that is important. There were times when I strove enormously for certain successes. I did not always achieve the goals I had hoped for. However, I accepted those realities. *Que sera. Que sera.* I'm not discounting my experiences, but I understand life's uncertainty, and I know we do not live in Ferdinand the bull's field with garlands of flowers draping our necks.

Someone living my early life could have been neurotic or extremely rigid. I was never accused of neither. Intense, driven, persistent, courageous—Yes. Judgmental—No. (Except once, when I refused to work with a father who was court ordered to my clinic and insisted he had the right to molest or even kill his daughters.) As a therapist, I accepted the beliefs and values of clients and helped them understand the source of their conflicts.

Life is full of earthquakes, of hurricanes, of people like my dad. My early life had prepared me for all of them. I did not know what waited for me beyond the mountain of my marriage, but I was confident that I could take it as it came. *I think I can, I think I can. I know I can, I know I can.*

Chapter Three

Just as my expectations for marriage were unrealistic, so were my expectations for divorce. Although I knew Neil would be hurt and depressed, I expected the routine of family life and career would stabilize his feelings of rejection. I had no idea how weak he was. When we were still together, other couples with whom we partied told me he would outgrow his drinking. When he came home late back then, I never considered that he might have had sex with one of the women at the bar. Later, my former sister-in-law told me she had sex with him when he was married to me. That possibility was unimaginable. When I talked to him after a drinking episode, he was always remorseful, a limp, castrated, sorry soul.

The drinking was not a daily event. It was intermittent, every few weeks. The rest of the time, Neil was cooperative, helpful, a partner, always loving me and complimenting my intellect. Because he had shared his back story with me, as I had shared mine with him, I understood why and how he was broken. His sisters called him Nellie. His mother had made him pee in an orange juice can in front of demeaning sisters. She took the violin away when he showed extraordinary interest and talent. In a way, Neil was my first case study.

Still, I left, and somehow, I expected him to be able to handle our separation. Two weeks passed. I saw the kids and still believed I could make this divorce work in a way I had not been able to make my marriage work. Then, the woman from whom I was renting told Neil the truth about Gene and me. Neil flew into a rage, and his rage converted to violence.

He got a lawyer. He got a gun. He tried to kill himself twice while wearing a two-hundred-dollar suit. That was the irony that was Neil. The poet philosopher turned villain.

First, he axed my life-size and half life-size sculptures, covering the street with fragments. He chopped up my 48-inch by 36-inch oil paintings and threw those in the street. Then he set fire to all the photo albums I had lovingly created during our courtship and sixteen-year marriage. It was a tiny campfire, yet it felt like an extremely painful inferno. It seemed he was destroying the wonderful part of those years as a family, but fortunately my children and I know better.

And then he upped the intensity of his anger. "I'm going to shoot him and you," he shouted on the phone.

Neil never found us, although he drunkenly sought out my faculty and fellow students. It was a great time for grad school drama. I met my children secretly two blocks from the house, not wanting to put them through his drunken rantings. I signed every agreement his lawyer put in front of me, including cognovit notes (whatever they were), bank accounts, and titles to cars and house. All I wanted was out.

The state required we attend counseling, and I began to understand that the weight of the marriage had always been on my shoulders. As I began to imagine what else was possible in my life, the euphoria went way beyond the sex I had with Gene. I could not believe how light I felt.

Universally, shit happens. When you learn it young, as I did, you blow it off, and you learn to live in the present, to not escalate the problem, to go see what else there is after the next bend in the road. That's what I did. It's what I do now, years later, even when I suffer great physical pain. I just go ahead and do it. I live with what is. I intervene when possible. I remain a person of active decisions, not always wise, but definitely not passive.

When I left Neil, I already understood that life is long, and I knew my sons and I would eventually be okay. I had not counted on Neil's unpredictable, horrific behavior, especially having left him with primary custody of our sons, a permanent professorship, two cars, two boats, and a two-story house on Centerport Beach. His erratic outbursts continued until 1975, when he remarried. In the meantime, he went to rehab, and I shared my new, free life with Gene, living in rented houses with and without other students.

Early on, we shared a windblown rickety four-bedroom farmhouse that hung on the edge of a cliff overlooking Long Island Sound with four grad students. Gene knew how to cook a steak and a potato in the shared kitchen with its thirty-two-gallon garbage can and large wooden picnic table. That was it. We slept on a beat-up old bed, had a crappy couch and one major bathroom, its toilet covered with pee on and around the bowl, and mold around the tub. Bugs crawled where unused soap bars moldered in puddles of water.

"I'm not the mother here," I reminded myself repetitiously. "Just wear my flip flops and manage."

I learned that I could survive in even these circumstances and be happy. I did teach Gene how to eat more than meat and potatoes. He became a stir-fry gourmet cook.

We negotiated how often to change the sheets. Both of us were involved. I was not the homemaker, but I did have standards, and four weeks of a hard-used bed was insupportable. We were both using those sheets, I reasoned, and we were both responsible for their condition when we got into bed. Ultimately, we changed the sheets every two weeks. Together.

I was a sex trophy for Gene. He wanted me to have eyelet shorts and see-through gauze blouses to draw more attention to his conquest—a beautiful, bright woman with a shoulder-length mane. He was in his mid-twenties, and I in my mid-thirties, a bit of a gap by the standards of the times, especially considering that I was a mother. To be divorced was acceptable, but being eleven years older was breaking the barrier. To avert boredom, I wanted to share activities other than sex with him, so I bought our first two tennis racquets at a garage sale. Within weeks, he exceeded my skill. Sex remained the heavy glue.

I also tried sailing with him, taking advantage of the ninety-eight-dollar Styrofoam sailboat the Kool cigarette company was selling to advance its brand. Our first outing, which was in the sound, was too much for Gene. He hated capsizing, swallowing water from uncontrollable waves, and then having to right the boat to get it to shore. Oh well. There was always sex.

Before Gene, I had never gotten drunk. Neil had mastered that activity, and I knew I had to be always available for our sons. With Gene, I didn't feel those restrictions. He taught me how to chug Heineken and burp outrageously. I lost the self-consciousness that had earlier prevented me from really dancing, and I got that reggae beat down pat. Neil had always danced a waltz or two-step with me. He could have danced anything, but he always chose the safe route and took me ballroom dancing. Gene took me club dancing, and with him, I learned to be comfortable without someone holding onto me.

The last place we rented, we opened to other graduate students. We needed one more renter and vetted a community college professor after meeting him at a neighbor's dinner party. True to Bob's lifelong search for his next conquest, he left the dinner party to follow me home. Gene was involved in conversation, so Bob pretended concern because of the deep snow. When he learned I wasn't interested, I told him then what I have told him all our lives, "I need a friend more than I need a lover." Un-rebuffed, he quickly went on to ask about renting and was thrilled to set up an interview for the house share.

You can learn a lot about someone by just visiting where they live, so we went to his place. The least amount of furniture possible: a floor mattress, a table, one chair, and a TV, reflected his enduring inurement to discomfort or pain. His refrigerator simply contained a frozen, broken, beer bottle and lots of ice. We quickly knew with whom we were getting involved, and rented him the mother/daughter portion of the house.

Bob became a lifelong friend, one of a kind, a fun-loving eccentric, who does his chores under friendly guidance and is now retired with full benefits. I still laugh when after announcing to us that he was running for the teachers' union presidency, he told us, "I am going to win."

"How can you be so sure?" I asked.

His reply. "I've been voting for all the professors who are on leave or out of the country." He acted mystified when Gene and I told him, "Stuffing the ballot box will get you fired."

Long before the "#metoo" generation, Bob, unable to ignore his many lovely female students, had many close calls with suspension by his administration. Once I caught him cavorting in the neighbor's backyard with a thirty-four-year-old student and had to forcefully say, "This is totally unacceptable. You do not look that good naked." He laughed.

Several memorable encounters occurred during our

shared trips to Europe. One night, traveling in his rather old diesel Mercedes, we arrived at 11 p.m. in Brugge, Belgium. The usual B & Bs were full-up. As usual, we had no reservations. The bar was still open, so the guys decided we would have a few drinks. I contained my discomfort. *This is not the time. There are no women here. We have no place to sleep.*

Although it was obvious three of us could not sleep well in one car, my companions appeared unconcerned. However, they continued to schmooze with the locals, asking if anyone had a room we might share. It turned out the barkeeper had been quiet about a room upstairs with two beds, usually not a rental. This is where we were happy to park our tired bodies, and I crawled in with Gene, only to discover, minutes later, Bob energetically jumping on our bed, joyously asking to be let under our covers. Now, this friend is handsome, well built, and looks a lot like Hemingway, but since his seductive efforts at that first dinner party, I've had to remind him more than once what I told him the first time he hit on me—"You're a friend." Laughing and pushing him away, I playfully, yet seriously fended him off. Gene wasn't much help, already half asleep, but I managed, and Bob, rejected as usual, returned to his bed. Nearly forty-five years later, he has never let up. It has become a game.

Another time, drinking beer in a German biergarten I was showing off my newly acquired language skills and again laughingly I said, "Dich ficken gehen." He turned bright red. This was his home country, and others would understand. He energetically shushed me.

At home, Bob was concerned he was not sufficiently endowed, and knowing we were "unusual" psychologists, he privately asked us to check him out. At a north shore beach on a night when fluorescent sea creatures fell off our dripping bodies creating a magic beyond our imagination, we examined him and totally assured him physically he could satisfy anyone. Later, he visited a few homosexual clubs hoping to increase his odds fifty percent. He was disappointed. He did not have the capacity to sexually enjoy men, but he tried, and as usual, we laughed at his innocence.

Whatever the reasons, Bob was always cheap, getting the most money out of any exchange. For example, instead of giving Gene a pair of used jeans, he sold them to him for fifty cents. Together, we bought Amtrak unclaimed luggage and "stuff" that never made it during shipment. Thrilled to go home with many pairs of fifty-cent tennis shoes, Bob was determined to get his money's worth. Coming off the court one day, I was alarmed to see the court unevenly patterned with bright, red blood.

"What's this?" I asked.

He casually replied, "Nothing. My feet won't stop bleeding because of my shoes." He refused to throw them out because they were still new.

Married to Neil, I did all the social planning. In contrast, Gene was a full participant in determining our social life, friends, and travels. Deciding to have a party, Bob, Gene, and I emptied the living room of clutter, brought in large Bose stereo speakers, and invited fifty people to a dance party. Basically, Gene was the organizer. Around 11 p.m., we were energetically drinking, dancing, talking, eating, and flirting. Gene had been dancing, and I wasn't paying much attention to what he or anyone else was doing. I was dancing with a classmate decked out in leather pants and vest made of a hairy animal skin.

He asked, concerned, if I had noted Gene's disappearance with his dance partner. Over the beats of loud music, I yelled, "It's not a problem. It's his body, after all, and he isn't taking anything away from me."

If that wasn't the beginning of our path to sexual

experimentation, which was not that unusual or shocking in those days, it was close to the beginning. It was Gene's body, after all. What he did with that was none of my business, even though it occurred in our own home. Gene and I were partners. He had freed me from a rigid life of expectation and responsibility. No, let me amend that. I had freed *myself* from that life. Gene was only the catalyst. And we all know what happens to the catalyst in the end. It does not change.

Gene's family in Ohio had an auto-tag renewal business. We'd visit them and then the huge outlet store in Elyria, where we bought piles of clothes for minimal dollars and argued over which were the tolerably sexy outfits. Outrageous fun came with being dressed by an admirer, a voyeur, and a vicarious exhibitionist.

Our sexual energy was so spontaneous that we had sex in the campus broom closet and on the kitchen sink of a rented faculty apartment. It was a sight to see because I always had great difficulty hoisting myself onto the counter, and my laughter at seeing our reflection in the kitchen windows did not help. Doing it upside down solved some of those logistics, another example of youthful creativity. Opportunities abounded. Even a 10:30 evening walk erupted into our surprising the night creatures of a wooded Catholic churchyard.

On Wednesday nights, we would party with friends at Jack's Backyard, a local bar. The rectangular shape of the bar made it easy for each of us to wander off to opposite ends of the room and talk to other people. Gene got off watching me flirt with guys, so there never was a conflict of interest.

One night, he wanted me to wear just my trench coat and no other clothes. On the way home, the mood hit, and, on a rural road, we did the deed leaning against the car. Another time we picked up a late night hitchhiker and took him home. Graveyards also provided adequate cover during an occasional evening walk. During the day, tired of studying, we walked the old Stony Brook woods and found a serviceable tree on which I could stabilize myself. Where and when we did the deed was part of the fun—a contest to find the next unexpected setting.

This new life was full of joy for me, full of freedom, and a celebration of a me I had never guessed existed. I didn't know where it would take us or me, for that matter. And I didn't care. Just as I had to learn I was smart and conscientiously completing on schedule all student assignments, I learned I was really beautiful and extremely sexual. *I had pussy power.* During those months, my gradual awareness of those realities coincided with, the fading of the halo I'd been hauling around all my life. The woman who had to be married to have sex was having sex with her lover before she filed for divorce.

Gene read magazines like *Playboy* and *Penthouse*, and we started contemplating the idea of swinging. We decided it wasn't cheating if it was open, and we had rules. We first visited Plato's Retreat, a swinging club, in Manhattan opened in the 1970s by Larry Levinson, a high school friend of Al Goldstein, pornographer and publisher of *Screw* magazine. It offered a heated swimming pool, sauna steam rooms, whirlpool baths, a bar, a buffet, backgammon, and plenty of areas for various types of swinging. Once, I even saw a greyhound, but chose to not enter that room

I took pride in Gene's considerable anatomy and how women were constantly accosting him. He walked around with a boner even after sex, and way before "the little blue pill." We would socialize with other swingers outside the club, and in some way, my transition from marriage and monogamy to this life with Gene was surreal. We became friends with several couples we had met through swinging.

She was an exotic dancer. He was her manager. At her club, Gene and the couple encouraged me to dance, and I did for one set and then seriously considered the income possibilities. If I chose to dance, my income would exceed all the usual streams of income accessed by graduate students. I knew I would enjoy the power and exhibitionism of dancing. However, I was not living my life to make money. I followed my existing plan. I wanted to control my own narrative and not get sidetracked from my studies. Also, I probably was self-conscious.

Because my life with Gene was open, I was free to look beyond the ostensible script of what is possible. In my academic life, I consistently switched major interests. I started with one specialty, female sexual arousal, and got into another, women's assertiveness training. My goal was never to get rich or say, "I did that." The goal was always to be engaged, learn all that I could in all dimensions that mattered to me, and to help others. At this time in my life, Gene mattered to me.

Each of us, at different times, had flashes of wanting to get married. Fortunately for both of us, we never had those flashes at the same time, because we were not and never would have been lasting partners. Furthermore, people aren't designed to be passionately married forever, and I knew that.

But I was destined to be a parent forever, and I cared about my sons. When I first left, Neil was out of control, and so were they. Aaron was using drugs and alcohol, partly because it was endemic to our local culture. I observed public school and university faculty, parents, and kids using. I believed Aaron used the drugs to deaden his emotional pain. Our family had unpredictably changed. A steadying activity for both sons was their teaching and participating in competitive sailing, with first, Lasers and J boats, and later sail boarding, wind surfing, and paddle boarding. School was not a priority.

Because he could not tolerate public school, Aaron finally agreed to attend Lewis Wadham's School, which offered an alternative education much like the Summerhill experiment in England. Aaron was gifted, and we hoped this upstate setting would isolate him from the drug community. It did not, but at least he graduated from high school. By age twenty-one, he had become a lifelong vegetarian and a non-user of any alcohol or recreational drugs. He eventually graduated with a master's degree, summa cum laude.

My relationship with my sons was important to me, and I was being stymied. Neil interfered any way he could. If I was visible, he would stand there with his arms crossed, yelling crude insults in front of the neighbors and the kids, making it difficult for them to even get in my car. I picked them up two blocks from the house whenever I could, and I did manage to be allowed to drive Aaron to driver's education simply because Neil had to teach. I drove an hour to pick him up and another half-hour to driver's ed. Aaron spoke to me in the car, rarely engaged and effectively withdrawn.

At the driving school, I knew he was running out the back door and getting stoned. I wanted every opportunity to be with him even if he was stoned. He had taken on his dad's anger, although he didn't express it that way. When I would call, he just wouldn't come to the phone. "Abandonment" became Neil's favorite word to describe my leaving, and Aaron, as an impressionable thirteen-year-old, believed it.

Kurt and I would take long walks around ponds in the woods or eat at affordable restaurants. I had no income other than my six-hundred-dollar stipend and semiannual internship funds. I drove Gene's car to make the hour drive, rewarded with Kurt's openness and affection.

I never badmouthed their father, and I called at least twice a week although I didn't always get through to them. I was patient. I was there. Their grandparents were very supportive and did share adventures with them, including a trip on a Mississippi riverboat.

When I think about those days, I remember what I always tell my patients, "Life is long. Things either get better or worse, but they rarely remain the same." The belief I shared was and is, "Choose your behavior as if you will remain engaged with the important people in your life twenty years from any painful moment in the present. Protect yourself; don't let anybody beat you up. Always keep the door open." In my dealings with my children, those thoughts kept me consistently proactive and engaged. Yes, I was shocked, hurt, and rejected. I missed them with a great emptiness, I had always thought of myself as the home manager, but I never realized how important those daily interactions were to me and to them. My philosophy kept me on a solid course of parenting.

When I was planning my escape, I had never imagined Neil trying to cut me out of their lives entirely. Neil had worshiped me and put me on a pedestal. I had never known the extreme personal changes that might occur if an alcoholic, dependent personality were truly stressed. Although I had watched his parents killing a fifth of Old Crow every night, I had no idea what was involved in alcoholism biologically and emotionally. My disgust resulted in a naive solution. *Keep yourself, your children, and Neil away from those grandparents.*

Without me, Neil wouldn't have gotten a Ph.D. He could not have handled the pressure. Sometimes, during a binge, he destroyed his 3x5 note cards, the results of weeks of research. With sobriety and my encouragement, he could start again. Throughout the marriage, I carried him. I didn't do it out of a sense of wifely duty. I did it because I was invested in that degree. I was working two jobs so he would one day provide sufficient income to support our family. Because he was a professor, our children would not have to pay tuition. Later, I would have free access to other advanced degrees.

I believed things would, over the years, even out. They did. Today, my sons and I have an excellent relationship. Kurt, influenced by upmarket living in Sarasota, Florida, followed a path that segued his identity far to the political right. Talking has always been easy for us even during those horrible early years of the divorce. Today, we can watch numerous news channels and discuss the values expressed by various economists, entrepreneurs, and talking heads. Our conversations are rich and clearly biased, ongoing debates without anger. On the phone, we also catch up on family in California, Ohio, New York, Connecticut, and Florida. Then there is our continuing interest in Apple products, travel, his bicycling competitions, new books, old books, boating, and the meaning of our lives.

Aaron does not have time for detailed conversations with Kurt and some of the values he supports. However, it is quite clear how much Aaron and Kurt care for and love each other. However, they just do not agree on some personal values. For me, it is each to his own, but I like learning how they came to think and arrive at their respecttive points of view. Aaron's family and I are close, sharing holidays, boating, and time with his youngest son, Cole, who was born with a missing gene and is severely developmentally disabled. Cole has lived in a care facility for eleven years and comes home for visits every two weeks. After the death of my second husband, I moved back to Long Island in 2006 to help with Aaron's family.

I am extremely grateful for my sons and a great eighteen-year marriage to my second husband. However, I will never regret leaving their father. I loved Gene, but love reflects the different dimensions of who we are. After all, how can you make contracts for emotions? When all this death-do-us-part stuff started, most humans were dying by age thirty-five, making it easy to lapse into a dream of eternal security and of being together "forever after."

That was not to be the case with Gene, though. Although he was not terribly kind and not terribly generous, he treated me like one of the guys, and that meant a great deal to me during the time we were together.

Chapter Four

Although Gene was never jealous of my friends or family, I soon found out he could be jealous if he wasn't able to be included in something I was enjoying sexually. We associated socially with some of the swinger friends we met at the club because they were smart and/or had interesting hobbies. One such couple, an MD and a nurse who worked with him, were attractive but not gorgeous individuals. We remained interested in them after the novelty of sex wore off because of our great conversations and food.

One night, when we were living on the North Shore, we had them out to Long Island for dinner at our two-bedroom cottage. The next morning, we headed out to the South Shore nudists beaches. We hung out on our blankets, and we enjoyed spending time with them. The MD had brought Quaaludes, which I knew nothing about. I took one, confident that this medical team could handle anything that went wrong. It was the first and last time I took that drug. It turned me into a limp, wonderfully warm dishcloth. I felt like pudding, and when it was time to leave the beach, I could not walk. My legs were like rubber.

Gene was driving the full speed limit on the expressway, so they would be on time to board the LIRR home to their jobs in Manhattan. The MD began fooling around with his companion, and I—on my one Quaalude—decided to crawl into the backseat and enjoy the action. Gene was not happy. I hadn't done anything against our rules. He just couldn't be in two places at once, and that frustrated him.

Another time, as an extension to meeting an unusual, bi-racial couple during a swinging experience, we were invited to their posh, Manhattan penthouse for a small party. Upon my arrival, the fully glassed living room ceiling and a group of exotic women impressed me. I watched the scene for a long time as I tried to decide what I wanted on this particular evening. The women occupied the greater part of the living room, forming a sculpture of multi figures, all diaphanous and beautiful. Although they were probably moving, to my eyes, they had created all the realities of a life-sized sculpture. And when I was invited to join, I did. We performed for ourselves and the audience.

Most of the guys were happy to just observe and be aroused. Being a young stud, tall, tanned, aroused, Gene was again not too happy. He wanted in on the action, and he was not invited. At that moment, however, I was enjoying being part of this drama, integrating shared human energy and affection. I did not worry about Gene.

Later in our relationship, Gene and I were at the home of another couple we had met in the groups, and although the home was nothing like the Manhattan penthouse secured with twelve-foot cyclone fencing, this average home contained a waterbed, my first—and what an experience that was. The four of us had a good old time of active heterosexual fun. After the guys drifted off, the woman and I started fooling around, but we were exhausted as well and fell asleep.

First light came. Birds were singing, and I really did

smell flowers on soft breezes. The woman and I awakened and passionately enjoyed ourselves. Then her husband woke and joined the two of us. Finally, Gene woke up angry. He had missed some of the action.

Gene achieved through cleverness and taking short cuts whenever possible. I achieved with hard work and persistence. My Ph.D. was three hundred pages. His was twenty-five pages. We graduated in 1977 and received two job offers for two Ph.Ds. in central Florida and Lubbock, Texas. We chose Florida and, after working there, I labeled it, "The Incest Capital."

After we arrived in Florida, a friend I taught with in Ohio housed us in her apartment for two weeks. Then we set up our first condo rental with Brahman cattle on one side of the building and gators on the other. We allowed the beauty of golf club greens to support our arrogant belief that we had truly arrived. With white carpet and a screened second floor porch without external access, our new home challenged us with dead love bugs creating an eight-inch border throughout the apartment. Vacuuming was a daily necessity during the love bug season.

One Sunday morning enjoying the privacy of our home, we planned to eat our breakfast on the porch without the bother of clothes. We opened the slider to the tightly screened porch, intending to also read the paper when a definitely aggressive snake lunged at us in an attack mode. Gene, assuming the manly role, balls shriveled, said to the wise older woman (me) "What should I do?"

Wise older woman said, "Hell if I know."

I knew about spiders, but my knowledge of snakes ended with the Pennsylvania "cottonmouths" my cousins bragged we had caught and killed. The three guys and I worked as a team, using snares and burlap bags, and later we disemboweled and mounted them on wooden boards. The rattler in Sumter County, Florida, was more active and smaller. We feared his aggression. Our solution: Gene was enlisted to use his precious tennis racket and a large plate. Gene had longer arms. He completed the task and delivered that critter to the condo manager, who confidently identified it as a rattlesnake and then took it off our hands.

Clinically educated staff in our new location were few and weak. The prior CEO had garnered federal money for buildings and staff to create a rural mental health center with three locations. Staff had limited experience with serious mental impairments, and before we arrived, the CEO, who had a background in business, felt he had to intervene in the hospital's psychiatric floor. A new patient was out of hand, so our memorable CEO put on a white coat, added a few pens in the pocket, spoke with faux-professional confidence, and told the patient to disrobe. Totally. The unlocked door proved a convenient escape route for the naked, out-of-control individual in the clinic's considered care. Down the two flights of stairs, out onto the street in a sleepy town he fled with a roll of toilet paper unfurling as he eluded the professionals. Police intervened.

This event preceded our arrival with a proper CEO and CFO. Gene became head of research and data collection along with clinical duties, and I initially headed the Family and Children's Unit, which included a twelve-bed facility and classroom and the outpatient clinic.

Gene and I presented to the community as married. We began managing our money. Our income was the same, and we put it into a common pocketbook. We didn't have *his* money and *my* money. If I wanted to give something to my children, I took extra work. When he complained about the cost of women's personal items or beauty products, I replied, "You always eat more than I do. We're even."

Gene and I had three significant moves in Florida as we were achieving and continuing to swing. Each house was bigger and better. The final one, located in Sweetwater

Oaks in Orlando, with two fireplaces and a cathedral ceiling, was perfect for us. Four years later, we moved because Gene was bored.

"You can go anywhere in the world," I said. "I'll come along."

Because of my lack of confidence at the beginning of my career, I had become licensed for both educational and clinical work—overachieving, that's for sure. I needed the certainty that employment was always available.

"Anywhere in the world," became Topeka, Kansas, where Gene was hired as a university professor.

Although I said I would follow him, I wasn't sure what I would really do after Gene left for Kansas. With a friend, I looked for and seriously considered buying a house in Orlando, where I now had roots. However, when Gene called, nearly begging me, he almost cried, "You promised. You have to come. You can't stay in Orlando." Again, he said "You promised me." Unfortunately, I'm a sucker for a friend in need. I've never been one to seek the aid of the white knight. If anything, I *am* the white knight, and even in work, my goal is to help people evolve. In 1981, I joined him in Kansas.

Soon after, he became involved with one of his graduate students. Predictable? Yes. Besides, he and I had no ties other than history and habit. Because of her resemblance to the actress, Brooke Shields, he called her "Brooke," and she was his first traditional girlfriend.

Ultimately, Gene and I outgrew each other. After six months in Topeka, I still couldn't find a permanent job. Friday night happy hour free appetizers became shallow and insignificant while Gene's faculty parties were just as boring as Neil's were on Long Island. I needed more challenging work and finally landed a big consulting job in Kansas City, sixty miles away. I thought we would be commuting on the weekends, or that he would get a full-time job at one of the several colleges in Kansas City But I assumed too much. He didn't make an effort, and I realized he considered the relationship over.

We were both active skiers, and I also assumed we'd be taking ski trips together after I moved to Kansas City. Instead, we took only one trip to Colorado, and it clearly was the end. He told me he was going to meet a woman and that he was going to be staying with her. Once we arrived, he dropped me off at the ski lodge and disappeared. That drop off was the beginning of my sexual adventures as a single woman. While there, I met three college kids from Idaho, and those young men and I shared meals, beer, and bed.

On the way home, Gene and I rode together, and he described the most recent conquest the way he did all the women in his parade—almost as if he were asking for my approval. I never saw him again, and the only times we spoke were occasional phone calls when he wanted my opinion regarding career changes, publications, women, and marriage. A year after our last ski trip, he married. Within five years, she divorced him. Once he called, asking me what I thought about his accepting a high-status job with a major northeastern university. During one of our catch-up conversations, he shocked me by saying, "I loved you. I do want you to know how important you've been to me throughout my life."

Later, Gene told me he had leukemia and was in an experimental study at Johns Hopkins. He was determined he was going to beat it with the power of his mind. The last time he called, I could tell he was failing. He was no longer the optimistic larger-than-life character I had loved. I learned of his death from friends who had known us during our Long Island years. The loss of our day-to-day relationship had not bothered me much, but the loss of this person and all that he stood for still brings me to tears today.

Gene died at age fifty-two with three cars, a Porsche 924, a truck, and another car he just could not pass up. He had two German shepherds, and he loved entertaining friends—as we had—by stir-frying meals in his wok. Bob, our enduring mutual friend, told me Gene confessed even to him that I was the most influential woman in Gene's life. This man went through women like bottles of wine. Out of all of them, I stayed the longest, ten years.

He was a major chapter in my evolution. Once he and I broke up after that final ski trip, I looked beyond the mountain again. I was restless and wanted to explore who I was without a significant man in my life. How and where would my love of freedom and unscheduled time materialize? Were my sex explorations simply a part of being with Gene? And how could my love of sailing be satisfied in the Midwest?

I shed some tears over the breakup, not because I wanted to stay with Gene, as he probably thought, or even wanted him to break up with Brooke. Although I knew his relationship with her would end, it had nothing to do with me. I shed tears because I was breaking away from the familiar. That I would miss.

I worked with a woman who was also going through a breakup, and we shared tea and tears, which aided my transition to becoming single after many years of first marriage, and then the ten Gene and I had shared. So, was I okay? I felt I was, but I also thought I should check in with the best therapist I could find. After all, I was a resource for other people trying to figure out how to improve their lives. I needed to figure out—and if necessary—modify mine.

I met with the psychiatrist and told my story. All of it. The marriage to and breakup with Neil. My love for my kids. The affair with Gene. The swinging. The desire to move beyond the mountain to sailing, somewhere, some way. I shared with this man everything I had done and felt, including my absolute lack of guilt. Then I asked for his opinion.

"Nita," he said. "You sound great to me, and you are the most unusual woman—except one—I've ever met. You're certainly adequate to be in this field."

For seven years, I pondered what it meant to be single. I asked myself, "Who is Anita without Gene? Without Neil?" This was the beginning of pushing the envelope further regarding how I wanted to live. I no longer needed to accommodate Neil, Gene, or the children. In 1982, I got serious about dating and wondered what I was going to do with myself. Outside my job, I didn't know anybody. But wait. I was still acquainted with people left over from my swinging days.

One couple, in particular, remained friends. He worked for Social Security, and she was a travel agent. When they traveled out of town for a week, I babysat for them. One night, I was visiting them, this time as a single friend of the family, and they told me about Tom Jones (not *that* Tom Jones), a dentist who wanted to be a swinger. Later that week, Tom and I got together as a threesome with the husband. We met at my apartment. That was our first date.

Tom seemed a perfect partner for me. At six-four, he walked around with a big pocketbook (in the 1980s!). He was gentle and slightly androgynous. Our evenings restored the fun to my sex life. An evening in might include us nude except for a rope of pearls around my neck and maybe a gold chain on his. We did make great use of the dental chair, a bright red one as I recall. It was just fun, that's all.

By this time, I knew I wanted to sail. Tom bought a twenty-four-foot sailboat, and I bought the motor so—should there be an end (and I always assumed relationships change)—I'd sell him the motor. We sailed and went bass fishing on the Lake of the Ozarks, an artificial lake in southern Missouri. Tom introduced me to an eighty-five-year-old woman who invited me to fish from her dock and brought me tea. I brought my recorder. Vivaldi's *Four Seasons* combined with the rippling water and the patterns of birds lifted me into the glory of oneness with nature.

A friend of a friend, my gynecologist, provided my annual exams and initially withdrew fluid from some of the painful fibroid cysts that were causing me breast discomfort. Finally, I asked her to stop, which she did. We occasionally met at the bar for a drink, and in 1983, after my annual pelvic exam, instead of patting me on the head and saying, "I'll meet you in ten minutes at the bar," she said, "I'm feeling uncomfortable without checking your cysts. Let me take some samples."

I complied, mounting her examining table, and offered my breasts to the needle. She extracted fluid from only three of the larger cysts (There were hundreds). Two were positive. The immediate referral to a cancer surgeon confirmed the need for removing the breast testing positive for lobular carcinoma in situ. In those days, I was a consultant at the Kansas City Medical Center, so I had access to all the latest research.(Again, these events all occurred before we had personal computers, and the libraries were our most up-to-date resources regarding research in specialized areas.) I learned this cancer usually reappeared in the remaining breast within five years. I did not want to live with that anxiety and determined to have both removed. After a bit of an argument with the surgeon, I prevailed. He agreed to a bilateral surgery.

Then another butting of heads occurred because of my having read too much—according to his point of view. I wanted implants to be put in place immediately after the breasts' removal. I figured going under one complete anesthesia was safer than waiting months to repeat the process. He argued this was not the "usual" treatment robotically stating, "Usually the breast tissue is totally removed, leaving a flap of skin for six months. Only then, will the plastics surgeon put in the implants."

I understood his reasoning was to make sure that all the cancer cells had been removed. However, this made no sense to me because cancer cells could not exist in breasts now in the discard bucket. Finally, I found a plastic surgeon who would stand by and after the initial general surgery, put in the implants.

A day later, wrapped in gauze bandages that felt like supportive armor, I returned to my apartment. Tom, now a committed friend, was waiting for me. On that very day, and with the bulky bandages, he caressed me and told me, "You are not your breasts. You are much more. I love you."

Then we made gentle love. I remember that afternoon with extraordinary vividness and feel tears of deep appreciation even at this moment more than thirty-five years later.

Despite our close friendship, I believed Tom needed to leave his dental practice in Kansas City and move to a less competitive small town. This he did, commuting to see me. I also drove the four hours to be with him and the twenty-four-foot boat. I wrote advertorial blurbs for the newspaper to signal to the community that a new dentist was in town. He joined the community theater, made new friends, and set up a more successful practice.

After one of our weekly sails, we had ratcheted the sailboat onto its trailer and parked it on the side of the road. It was almost ready to be hauled home.

I had to go to the bathroom, so I said, "Don't move the boat until I return."

Innocently, he thought he would surprise me, and he definitely did. He had pulled the boat only ten feet when power lines and tree branches snagged the mast, wrenching the base out of the deck. His enthusiasm cost him a several thousand dollar repair. I felt sorry for him, but his decision to go ahead in parking the boat was consistent with his sometimes childlike personality. He could not be a life partner for me.

Chapter Five

I was learning. Despite feeling bad for Tom, I thought *This is not my problem. I cannot always be helping him. I did not want to be in charge of his life.* His carelessness forebode behaviors that could be dangerous. I clearly understood we would not be a long-term match, but simply two friends who were very fond of each other. Nonetheless, Tom was fun, and I missed him. After I was out of the picture, he met an English teacher, and they became permanent mates.

In those seven years, Tom was the only one with whom I went swinging. I was casually looking for diversion from an intense workload with romance and other social activeties. I attended cultural events on my own, including jazz and folk music in restaurant basements, and chamber music or symphonic performances in the cultural center. One Valentine's Day, I teared up as I listened to Howard Hansen's Romantic Symphony (No. 2). During the intermission, I met a man wearing a Kansas City Royals silky, sky blue baseball jacket. I later visited his horse ranch, but other than a shared Valentine's dinner, we had little in common and did not meet again.

In the early eighties in Kansas City, my efforts to self-actualize influenced many of my choices. I began to accept the reality that I truly was becoming less encumbered by the expectations of others. I enjoyed the work in the clinic, in my private practice, as well as unfettered dating, and cultural events. I became aware I craved an academic challenge and did something about that hunger as well.

True to this increasingly secure self, I chose to make a modest change in my work schedule, asking the clinic coordinator of my day job, for a half-day off so that I might attend a graduate course in literature at the university. A course in the writings of Gabriel Garcia Marquez fit my available time and hence, without a reason except that I wanted to learn something absolutely different, I became enamored with his work. This interest grew and later expanded my awareness and exposure to other South American writers.

Through a friend of a friend, I met a group of two teachers and a social worker. I organized a night dancing in cowboy boots at the local cowboy bar. Predictably, that crowd was not our type, but we had fun learning the dance styles. We absolutely had no interest in returning to that club after learning the night after our outing, there had been a fight and a murder at the entrance to the bar.

The Zircon Ball was another kind of diversion from our professional working days. This ball was a fundraiser for abused women, and we were to come in elegant, dated and used Salvation Army evening gowns. Our dates were to wear suits from a distant past. One of us even had a feather boa while a few garish zircons drew attention to our slender necks or found a place in our carefully styled upsweeps. The women liked our plan but, as one of them asked, "What about the dates? We have no men in our lives." My answer? "We're wearing fake finery and fake diamonds.

We may as well have fake dates." I knew five unattached guys who were thrilled to play in the charade. One was gay. The others included a diamond merchant, a teacher, a craftsman in wood, and an accountant, each one looking for his own diversion. We now had dancing partners and were pleased to show up in full regalia.

Another night out, pushing myself to leave the predictability of evening television in my apartment, I met a good-looking housepainter. The hook for me was that he was also a poet. He always carried his poems with him. We read some of them at the bar. There wasn't much else to attract me to that man, and after one other meet-up at that same bar, we drifted apart with no physical intimacy. This may sound strange from someone who had enjoyed swinging, but now my life involved a different kind of choosing. I had clearly become much pickier knowing that men, many men, were usually available if I wanted to waste my time. The seduction routine and my need for pussy power was sated. I knew we women are the gate-keepers.

A friend, returning from a medical conference, telephoned and said, "We have to have lunch." We met the next day.

Alarmed, he starkly stated "Casual sex for us and our patients must absolutely cease. AIDS is a killer. Increasing diagnoses link it to a world epidemic."

With that, I changed my dating style, suggesting to my dates after a passionate kiss, that we put a notch in our belts, go home, and assume we had done the deed.

Around that time, I continued building a social network having nothing to do with developing a professional referral network. I just needed ordinary friends. I met two at the Kansas City Ski Club, a group that held parties in the city and organized chartered bus trips to Vail or Aspen. On one of the trips, I hooked up with Marla, a single MD practicing in a small town near Kansas City.

Ron, a sensible, stable electrical engineer, met the two of us on his first ski trip and thought he was in Candy Land. Recently abandoned by his wife, he thrived on the attentions of two good-looking, physically active single women. Marla and I taught him to ski. He diluted any sexual intensity by always being quite serious and teaching us facts like "Microwaves are not dangerous," and offering to wire our homes with security cameras.

Naive in the methods of courtship, Ron did not know how he might court Marla. I did. He listened to my wisdom and followed through. Within six months, I hosted their engagement party. As I write this book, they have been married for forty-five years.

Meanwhile, Marla invited me to drive with her to Aspen where we could ski and she could acquire continuing education credits. We checked into the lodge, skied that first day, and after dinner, we partied in the hot tub with a team of ER docs joking about races they had won and who would be injured this trip.

Ten years of self-taught skiing, successfully negotiating green slopes and winning a bronze medal in one of the club's competitions, put me in the mood to take my first skiing lesson. I wanted to increase my competence in skiing the blue slopes of Aspen—and racing.

The next morning, I arrived first at the top of the mountain to practice. I hopped off the lift into new powder that was not yet grooved by the expected crowd of racers. I saw the route, remembered the lesson, *to accelerate, keep my weight in the back of the boot.* I pushed off. Ignorant of ice that had formed during the night under the new snow, my enthusiasm obliterated the forthcoming reality. Ten gates later, I had torn my ACL (anterior cruciate ligament) and the ski patrol was carefully guiding the seven-foot rescue sled down the mountain to Aspen Hospital. A surgeon qualified to treat injured Olympic competitors waited.

Marla drove me home, and five weeks later, I was still driving my secretary's automatic car with my left leg navigating the gas pedal and brake.

Another friendship, albeit short term, was with a second *Kansas City Star* editor. The first one I had met through swinging. I met the second in the lobby of the concert hall. This journalist was paid to evaluate and write about concerts, plays, movies. He said he always had tickets for two.

He called for a date two nights later. I told him I was busy with work and didn't have time to date.

"You need to eat," he replied. "I'll bring you home-made potato soup." This he did within the hour. The soup was great, and so was he. I didn't get much work done that night.

A week later, we had brunch with Sloan Wilson, author of *The Man in the Gray Flannel Suit*, and his wife, Betty. His best-selling autobiographical novel, which became a 1957 film starring Gregory Peck and Jennifer Jones, examined the danger of corporate conformity. Long before *Mad Men*, both novel and film showed how the demands of the corporate world threatened traditional roles of marriage and family. *A Summer Place*, another book by Wilson, was made into a film starring the hot young stars of the time, Troy Donahue and Sandra Dee.

Unfortunately, Wilson's alcoholism made him an arrogant and unpleasant brunch partner, and that was our last encounter. Once I saw the editor interacting with Wilson, I realized that he, too, was arrogant. My date was also disrespectful of Betty and me and dominated the conversation. That brunch was our last date. There's sexual attraction and then there's knowing the person. I didn't really know the editor until that lunch.

Work was always interesting because I always said "yes" to whatever projects the clinical director suggested.

Federal money was still available for mental health clinics, and I wrote an outreach proposal allowing me to focus on early teenage pregnancies, prostitution, and high school dropouts. Working with the Kansas City Police Department, we decided that in addition to the normal court-ordered group therapy, we would make a video of how the hookers worked, who they were, and what eventually happened.

I role-played the prostitute, and my social worker provided the john, a young friend of hers. Cameras rolled, I sauntered, and we got horny. Our first and only time revealed the man's utter loneliness and need for a friend. For a while, I indulged him, playing monopoly and sharing an occasional meal as I gently encouraged him to join other groups and to realize what I already knew—that I was not a match for him.

At the Unitarian Universalist congregation, I met my best Kansas City female friend, Jennifer, a widowed dermatologist with three spoiled teenagers. At our first meeting, the sixteen-year-old twins were throwing strawberries during a formal dinner in her dining room groomed with large pieces of modern sculpture. Her husband's early death did not deaden her desire for a full life. She was well read, and she had enough money to support the arts. For more than a year, she sponsored a composer as he wrote his new opera. The score did not come to fruition, and based on his personality, I would not have bet on him, but she cared.

Another example of Jennifer's generosity was her pro bono skin care for patients who could not pay. We shared many conversations about the books we were reading and our thoughts about the liberal politics of our day. Sometimes, we booked a table and enjoyed listening to late night jazz at City Lights.

Together we played high-brow elite in the inner circle

of movers and shakers, but we also squatted and camped in the state parks. Sailing in a Sunfish rental, we were over-powered by the wind and wonderfully rescued by two on-leave army privates. They towed us to shore, and we four garnered protection from the storm by sharing a blanket over our heads and bodies.

Shivering, we gradually shed the cold, wet clothing. I have no idea who started it, but later that night, representa-tives of the United Sates Army joined us in our smallish tent. We shared breakfast the next morning. That was the end of my thinking my new friend was a staid, predictable doctor.

She invited me to a catered party at her house on the lake, and there again, we met eligible bachelors, including Damon. His wide, fleshy cheeks were charged with a pink glow, possibly generated by alcohol. His hair was thinning, he was acceptably overweight, and quickly revealed a gentle and caring soul.

"I saw your picture in the *Star*," he said. "I wanted to meet you but was afraid to track you down. I didn't want you to think I was a predator finding beautiful marks in the newspaper. But may I call you now?"

"Of course," I said, and gave him my number.

Needless to say, Sunday, the next day, we were flying in his four-passenger plane and sharing our backgrounds and interests. Damon was a serious player. He had a ranch with three riding horses because his daughters were "crazy" about horses, one wanting to train them, the other wanting to just be around them and have lots of horse dolls and sculptures.

His background was as varied as my own. Initially an engineering professor, he became a Ph.D. psychologist at a different university, and by the time we met, he was a practicing physician. To further my admiration, he played classical piano on a full baby grand and took me to upscale wine tastings. On those occasions, I always seemed to wear white, pushing my envelope. Other dates and a steady relationship followed. We had season tickets to the University of Kansas Jayhawks basketball matches, which we raced to after a half-day's work Saturdays, completing the week's scheduled clients. When we left the office, we shared a complete detachment from our working lives.

Realizing Damon and I would not become more intimate, I went on to other candidates. I was now seeking a lifelong romantic partner. When I became a temporary caretaker of my niece and nephew in order to give my brother Dick and his wife living on Whidbey Island, Washington, time and space to figure out why they were always fighting, I created another problem.

My one-bedroom apartment was definitely too small, so Dick asked Damon if he would rent two bedrooms and house share with Dick's children and me. This was a business agreement, and we, the renters, agreed to manage the kitchen clean up. Damon insisted on doing the cooking. He was the sloppiest gourmet cook I ever knew with counters in chaos and flour covering the floors. Two dogs, a great Dane and a German shepherd, tromped through the house at will, swinging their tails and fearlessly stepping on my bare feet. They easily added to the overall confusion, and it's a wonder we could ever catch up cleaning the rest of the house.

We rode Damon's horses, brushed, and fed them as well. He would watch my teenagers as I took art classes, giving away all my "masterpieces," only to rediscover them on visits to friends' houses years later. Damon's children, during their legally guaranteed visits, shared activities with mine. I had hoped for a rekindling of our initial romance. However, he had been seriously broken after a sixteen-year marriage when his wife came out as a lesbian and divorced him. As I came to know him better, I realized he was a masochist, and if his wife hadn't left him for another woman, he would have found another way to be misused. His dream—and it was a dream—was to meet and marry a wealthy woman so that they could buy a vineyard. A wine connoisseur, he constructed a personal $25,000 wine cellar and loved spending the money he did not have on new harvests here and abroad.

We had a no-smoking rule in the house. One day, when a guest entered, I called down the stairs, "We're not smoking here in this house." Damon was furious. It wasn't my job to announce house rules to guests. Damon went out of his way to be kind to people. He avoided conflict. During those six months, I kept my apartment, and my brother paid for the rent at Damon's.

Damon believed he wanted to marry but never took the risk. The psychiatrist I described earlier, the one I saw because I wanted to be sure I was someone who should be counseling others, encouraged me to be me when he said I was quite qualified and appropriate. He also told me something else. When I described my relationship with Damon, the psychiatrist told me my love interest would probably never get past his pain. That meant our relationship was as committed as it was going to get.

Once my brother's children returned home to Whidbey Island in the Puget Sound, my time with Damon lessened, although we remained friends. When I heard of his death recently, I reflected on our relationship and was filled with fond memories for the time he cared for me and went out of his way to be good to my brother's children.

The experience of loving someone who was unable to commit reminded me that true commitment requires focus and intent. Although for a short time, Damon had focus, looking back, I can see that he never had intent. Gene, who at various times considered marriage to me (as I did with him), had intent, but he rarely had focus. If my life were a piece of fabric, or to borrow from Carole King, a tapestry, which in many ways it was and is, Damon would be an ever-present thread.

Chapter Six

Hustling referrals for my psychology practice, I met a female attorney who after talking to me a while, said, "You're so gorgeous, Anita. You need to meet this bank president who's looking for someone like you to accompany him to professional events."

He was lean, attractive, a gentleman, and a good escort. We went to a christening, a wedding, and he took me with him as his date to elaborate parties, and one banquet. Although well recognized and well reputed, this man didn't exactly keep a clean home. He slept on crummy pillows. Here he was, at age forty-two, the youngest bank president in Kansas City, and he didn't even notice that some things in his home were just too gross to maintain.

He embarrassed me when he expected me to laugh at his silly imitations of Kermit the frog. I knew we had little in common when we began spending less time together. However, I did call him and asked him to meet me for fifteen minutes. I wanted to know if he had any awareness of our mismatch. He had no understanding. I provided the trite explanation, "We are not on the same page," which was to the point and unfortunately quite true. There was no chemistry.

My chronic restlessness had always led me to my next adventure, and now that I had experienced life on my own as a professional woman, I again wanted something new and different. Life had to be more than achieving, more than the prescription I had absorbed as a young woman. Motherhood, hanging with professionals, being one of those professionals, earning money, loving, and playing could not be the end of my life's experiences.

As always, Anita the problem-solver, started to think about how. *How do I make more personal time available? How do I reduce my workload?* A good idea, but my days were always measured by the employer. *Go for another degree?* I had already climbed that mountain, and I was no longer interested. I wanted something else. *Another love?* No one was forthcoming. *Studio art?* No, that wasn't right either. I decided to travel my continent accepting the label of "A Seeker," given to me by a Colorado lover. Please note, as I continued to explore the many choices of a now unfettered life, I had no intention of giving up my sexual pleasures. I was taking control of that quite personal dimension without the traditional understanding of "I love you" or "Are you committed to me forever?"

First, I tried taking a leave of absence. I kept the health insurance and moved my furniture into Damon's third-floor attic. I traveled east to west and north to south, to be with family and friends, sitting literally on the mountains, hiking, fishing, sometimes painting and drawing, always reading, never writing. I often slept in the car, sometimes in my tent. A second six-month leave of absence proved I wasn't coming back to the predictable lifestyle I had known so well. I was on the road without a mailing address. Lonely? Yes. Tired? Yes. This kind of living was definitely work.

Maintaining a daily inventory of food and water created stress. Decisions on destinations were not always obvious. There was no one with whom I could argue. Driving in Canada on an interstate highway, I could not find a bathroom. Finally, I parked on the berm and climbed up to a worker's abandoned portable toilet, precariously perched on boulders. When you have to go, you have to go, with or without spiders or snakes. Remember, those critters were childhood interests, so they were not troublesome. And may I add, today I would've just squatted at the side of the road and let the car horns howl.

I was on the road without a mailing address or phone. When I returned to Kansas City for the third time, I realized it was time to stand strong and alone. I had to give up my commitment to a professional life in order to create time to be.

I quit. No partner, no apartment, no health insurance, and always paying cash, I lived on my savings. For me, this was another leap out of my comfort zone. I experienced a different kind of anxiety but shortly got used to it. If my car was my home, I needed a different plan for each day. I never knew where I would spend the night unless I called ahead of time to see if a friend or family member wanted an overnight guest. Again, these telephone calls were not easily accessible. Pay phones in the wilderness are not common. If I stayed more than two nights I was either working or paying rent. Taking advantage of friends was and is not my style.

Once, I stayed a couple of months with past neighbors Ed and Joyce. It was fun to arrive with the guest room stacked with clippings and books they knew I would appreciate. Each of them held impressive administrative titles with IBM and the State of Florida. They also owned a swinging club in Florida. Now, they were helping me with computer technology, so I could obtain contracts for town hall talks and/or psychological testing. I still retained my licenses in Missouri, Florida, and New York. To this day, when I visit, there are always stacks of articles and books to share. I had their house key with an open invitation to come anytime, expected or unexpected. Upon arriving, often hungry, I would toast bread in the predictable Anita style, burnt. Craig, their son, would come in and call out, "Anita's here. I smell her toast."

Ed got a vicarious kick out of one of my small intrigues. Attending a talk about adventure travel in Argentina, I was keen to meet Buzz, the six-foot lean, well-muscled tour guide/travel agent. After he ended his lecture, I flirted with him.

"I'm very interested in your travels," I said, leaving the word, *interested*, vague.

Buzz invited me to a gathering in his apartment after the library talk. Probably twenty people poured drinks at the one piece of furniture in the kitchen, a drafting table. A foam mattress on the floor served as the only other accommodation to comfort. A few nights later, he called at 11 p.m. and invited me to join him in an expensive hotel room a friend had donated for the week. A half-hour later, as I walked low-lighted passageways surrounded by the bougainvillea and palm trees, I could feel the dampness of this artificial jungle and hear the frogs almost drowning my cautious footsteps.

Buzz had brought a suitcase filled with cans of vegetables and soup. He offered me the food. Bewitched, I learned of his dream to climb El Chatlen in Argentina's Parque National Los Glaciares the next month on his fiftieth birthday. He proudly showed me his new state-of-the-art crampons, which are hiking shoe adapters for climbing volcanically derived igneous rocks. His interest in women paled compared to his admiration for the men who also lived to climb mountains.

After that night, Ed often teased "Buzz really gave you

a buzz, didn't he? When will you see him again?"

He never called and I never sought him out.

On the road again, I sometimes I slept in my car at the side of the curb. I always picked a quiet neighborhood where traffic was minimal. I searched for a place without streetlights that inconveniently glared through my CRV's windows, which did not have curtains. Of course, auto repair shop lots, places behind billboards, or Walmart parking lots provided other options. I never stayed in highway rest stops because they were noisy, and I felt I would be conspicuously in danger. Sometimes I washed at a truck stop or in an inland lake (with environmentally safe soap) or at a campsite.

As far as campgrounds were considered, I had a choice between the luxury of modern plumbing or primitive outhouses that guaranteed there would be fewer people. I had my choice of private campgrounds or national or state or Army Corps of Engineer campgrounds, and I never once paid for a motel, let alone a hotel. I had enough of expensive hotels when I was a temporary consultant to various state/federal projects.

One time I arrived at a relatively empty campground, and because it was the end of the season, only one ranger was in charge. Strong winds blew through the grounds, and when he came to check me in, he found me struggling with my dome tent, which kept blowing away and resisted all my attempts to anchor those curved exterior stakes. He said he would come by after he closed the office and help me.

He did, and because he was off duty, I offered him a beer. No hanky-panky. Accepting that, he offered me a swim in the gated lake, which I accepted. I needed to wash. There we were on a very dark night without our flashlights, standing by the shoreline completely dressed. Not planning such situations, I wondered *What is the thing to do?* We disrobed. He finished his beer. We truly enjoyed the warmth of that water in contrast to the continuing wind.

Then we kissed. Returning to the campfire, we crawled into the tent and put ourselves to sleep. We slept through first light, and then he awoke and dramatically cried, "Oh my gosh. What time is it? My mother is really going to be worried. I'm missing church."

He grabbed his clothes and departed in a hurry.

Loneliness, excitement, and the unknown filled each day. I remained engaged but knew I was getting close to making another change.

Now, it was time to take real action exploring my passion to sail.

Besides the two men in Kansas City who bought boats in order to spend long weekends with me, I met others who truly loved sailing. My time in Florida renewed my acquaintance with two sailing couples. One couple met me Wednesdays after work at the boat dock on Lake Monroe, a small inland lake all of nine-feet deep. The shallowness allowed unexpected winds to ruin a quiet evening sail. I only somewhat enjoyed those meet-ups because we were not truly challenged and not going anywhere. On the other hand, my swinger neighbors, from Sweetwater Oaks had a Catalina 24, and they were thrilled I could join them. Totally unsure of their sailing skills (I had just taught the husband to swim two years prior), I suggested we day-sail to various destinations north and south of Cape Canaveral, and we did.

I believe they really needed me. Once, when we were a quarter mile offshore, we looked down into the galley and saw that the floorboards had come loose and were floating in three inches of water. I went down the ladder through the main salon to find them banging against the side berths. The whole place smelled like a toilet.

"What should we do, Anita?" the husband said. "Call the Coast Guard? Put on the life jackets?"

I, the hero of the day, determined the thru-hull plugs were in place, and turned the on-off water intake valve. Their mechanic eventually solved that problem. It was only a cracked hose.

Another time, the engine stalled and then, completely stopped, refusing all efforts to restart except for momentary groans. By elimination, we noted a one-inch rope wrapped around the propeller. Neither of my friends are strong swimmers. With the boat floating free, I was elected to put on my flippers and diving mask and use my strength to cut that line. They were excellent cheerleaders, and again, I was their hero.

Despite the pleasures of day-sailing, I knew I was not moving forward on my true goal— long-term sailing, a total change in lifestyle. I wanted to travel oceans, permanent destinations unimportant. So how could an experienced professional in teaching and counseling make this happen? The psychologist in the back of my head said, *Do something. It may not work, but try. You have only one life to live. Quit stalling.*

Because of that thought, I took a totally divergent path. Not feeling restricted to the blue-water sailing goal, I changed plans and decided to follow my brother Daryl to Guatemala City, where he was taking courses in economics and philosophy. He had been in contact with my parents, then living in Florida. He offered to help me, if I so desired, to settle in Antigua, Guatemala.

I understood this area was far more accessible and safer than the big city, and he would find me a dollar-a-night room with one bed and one chair in one of the international backpackers' quarters. I met many permanent residents who introduced me to their friends and families — an attorney, a Canadian union organizer who owned the local bar, a couple born in Connecticut raising their children in Antigua, and a beautician who dyed my hair without running water. I ate dinner in their homes. We attended football games where some of them competed. We drove to the area's largest market and the church in Chichicastene-ago. Imbedded in its past, many pre-Christian ceremonies threaded through the Catholic services. On market day, I shopped the cobbled streets and bought heavily wool em-broildered *huipiles*, which I later converted to exotic sofa pillows.

A week later, our group drove to Lake Atitlan, where activists against the Vietnam War from the 1960s still camped and danced along the shore. During ensuing weeks, I thoroughly enjoyed the image I had assumed. I lived as a fearless actress taking on roles for days and sometimes weeks. I felt as if I had disguised all vestiges of my past identities, and I indulged my creativity and became another person. I was involved in marketing jewelry for the husband of a new acquaintance. Their shop required someone who could sell sensitively designed silver adornments to much needed buyers.

One morning I was driving an acquaintance to the airport in Guatemala City. Traffic slowed as we neared the congested city, and the car in front of us stopped. An attractive Guatemalan, dressed in suit and tie, left his driver at the wheel of the car with the engine running. He decisively walked toward me and without a pause, reached through my window and handed me a long-stemmed red rose. Smiling he said, *"Eres tan bella. Por favor llamame."* He handed me his card, which identified him as an attorney, and then, he quickly returned to his car.

My friend excitedly said, "Call him. Why not? He should be interesting and he apparently has money."

I never called but have often wondered if this was unusual behavior or part of his daily routine. His superior taste in women (especially me) and the gift of the rose hinted at a romantic possibility. Women who responded to his initial outreach would have been automatically screened for their capacity for adventure.

On the other hand, I still prefer to believe that he happened to be bringing a bouquet of roses to his business associates, and after watching me for a few miles as our cars traveled slowly side by side, he impulsively decided to take a rose from the wrappings and give it to me.

I met an importer, a Colorado émigré who was a broker for Guatemalan manufactured clothing. Quite willing to change my roles in life's ever-changing reality, I donned a proper white blouse, pinned my hair into a bun, and became his clipboard-carrying assistant. He made the appointments with manufacturers and rented a car. We drove to small plants in the city or small towns where there were sometimes twenty and sometimes only two women with sewing machines. We accepted luxurious samples representing big-name designers, and I was smiling and pleased when he gave me the few he did not need for sales in the states.

This was a place for dreamers, those who sought lives different from their previous ones. One CEO of a mental health center in Texas involved me in shopping for a suitable structure to house a twelve-bed orphanage. We finally settled on a building, without running water, not far from the main road. We made the decision to pay for day labor to pump all the water because town water was expensive. We parted company when he returned to Texas to buy mattresses and other necessities not easily available in Antigua. He used his own savings.

Probably my most unusual acting role developed when I met Sanzin waiting in the single checkout line of a small grocery store. He, German born, and now a Guatemalan citizen, chatted briefly and to my surprise, asked, "Would you be interested in helping me develop a business growing and exporting roses to the states?"

He must have intuitively recognized my adventurous

spirit. Although I knew nothing about rose ranches, I was eager to learn about writing initial proposals, obtaining venture capital, identifying fertile, well-managed farms, and finally establishing export and import connections. He would not pay me, but he would house and feed me, and that sounded like a reasonable exchange.

Returning to the hostel to pack my clothes, I told some of my Guatemalan acquaintances what I was planning, and they were shocked, stating "Sanzin has never invited anyone to his ranch." "He is a recluse." "Tell us what he and his house are like when you return because he has remained a mystery for years."

As Sanzin and I drove forty-five minutes up a small mountain, I noted the narrowing road becoming a winding driveway carefully designed and planted with palms, bougainvillea, daisies, and hibiscus. I studied the Guatemalan and Mexican sculptures standing two- to six-feet tall as we followed the path and then entered an opening in the jungle canopy.

Then, I paused in wonderment as he stopped the car. I breathed deeply. I marveled at the lines, the beauty of his house, modest in size, yet a masterpiece of architectural creativity akin to Philip Johnson's designs. Later, I learned Sanzin had been an award-winning, internationally successful architect. A Japanese award for designing and supervising the construction of an earthquake-resistant comercial building hung in his office. I then understood that this house was designed to withstand the area's many earthquakes. The reasons for the independent modules, loosely connected by walkways and moving bridges, made sense. I also learned why he and his wife had moved to Guatemala. They were no longer interested in the competitive world of German enterprise.

Each morning I prepared fresh fruit contrasting its sweetness with the bitter Guatemalan coffee that we savored under the Banyan tree. Like royalty, Sanzin and I sat on hand-carved seats. A tree, sawed through the center, was beautifully carved and served as the table. Seated at the table, I watched the maid working in the different modules. She hummed as she walked between hanging flowerpots and the pasta draped and drying over horizontal broom handles.

I felt sad as I watched her work, recalling Sanzin's previous day's story when he explained why his wife had permanently returned to Germany. Shortly after he built a rough layout of their new home, one of the many random uprisings by revolutionaries erupted. Sanzin, returning home, seeing an armored vehicle in his driveway, abandoned his jeep, and hid in the brush, squatting low to the ground, fist to his mouth. He teared as he described his feelings of helplessness as he watched the guerrillas raping his wife and maid. I teared as I heard his story, feeling his guilt and helplessness.

Sanzin identified as a colonialist, represented the wealthy, the enemy protected by the repressive military of the "democratically elected" government. The Mayan and Ladino peasants were the revolutionaries fighting for universal democratic rights and representation. The civil war, begun in 1960, had never stopped, and the outrageous differences between the rich and the poor continued to foster violence such as that rape of his wife and servant.

Later, when I was driving a rental car, I was stopped at military checkpoints, and my stomach tightened as I provided my passport and tried not to stare at the machine guns. Before my time in Guatemala, my closest experience with civil war was the continuing race violence in the states, but this occurred in other neighborhoods, not where I lived. During the mid-sixties when the riots were flaring throughout the states, my house cleaner hid herself and her children under their bed in the Cleveland ghetto.

The aromas and colors of freshly ripened fruits, including citrus, melons, berries, and mangoes, made my job of preparing breakfast a pleasure. My primary work with Sanzin was uneventful. I typed his dictated proposals in English because the interested venture capitalists were usually bilingual Guatemalans. We met them in town in a rented, ground-floor, crudely painted, unfurnished room. Sanzin had brought in a table with sufficient chairs so they could read and discuss the plans. We visited ranches actively growing roses. There I learned about humidity, establishing workable irrigation systems, fertilization costs, and which plot designs produced the best yields.

Returning home late one evening, I continued to appreciate the beauty of the place. Lanterns lit the patios so that night light reflected the colors of hundreds of inverted glass bottles. The sounds of the gently moving wind chimes interrupted my thoughts about rose ranching.

We ate supper in the living room, and I studied photos of his previous work and his recent ink drawings representing modern myths. I breathed the harmony of the universe as I looked through the room's wall-to-wall window opening to the galaxies above and the city lights fifteen miles below. Listening to Brahms, we enjoyed each other's company and then we enjoyed our bodies on a blanket and pillows we had arranged on the living room carpet. Suddenly, the ground rumbled. The ground shook, and I thought *What a man!* About to scream with inevitable satisfaction, I definitely was not inclined to disrupt my pleasure. I was reaching with both hands trying to grab the earth. I struggled to breathe and calm my racing heart. I did not realize the intensity of that orgasm was actually integral with the movement of the planet. We did not stop as the earthquake intensified. We might have died at that moment. Dare I ask, "What a way to go?"

Looking back now, the experience is amusing. In that

singular moment I realized some situations are beyond control. *Why give up a perfectly good orgasm for an earthquake I could not stop?*

Chapter Seven

Shortly thereafter, I returned to Clearwater, Florida, and placed a personal ad in *Cruising World*. Because I was paying by the line, I cut to the chase and hung bait: *Beautiful Ph.D. psychologist seeks blue water sailing. Call xxx xxxx or write xxxxxxxx.*

Wow. I had discovered the formula. The phone began ringing before I was out of bed.

Letters of intent, or as I called them, "applications," were so numerous that I compressed them into an eight-inch stack under my bed. I was thrilled with the approximately fifty opportunities I might consider.

My dad read some of the applications and raised an eyebrow over the guy who wanted to lick between my toes. As you can see, it was relatively easy to initially screen-out unlikely captains.

I spoke with candidates on the phone, asking directly, "What is your agenda? Why are you calling me? Are you looking for a bed partner, a cook, or someone to share a long-distance journey?" Because I am expert interviewer, we could cut to the chase, and if an initial fit, we arranged a safe time and place to meet, eat, and talk. If vibes continued to be comfortable, I asked to go aboard the yacht. (Sensitive captains never call their boat, *a boat*. It is always *a yacht*).

One day, at seven in the morning, I answered a call to my parents' phone, and heard a male voice say, "Marry me." Shocked, I didn't respond immediately.

"Who is this?" I asked.

He explained that his name was Paul, and he was an executive with a manufacturing firm, looking for someone to join him in sailing offshore. We agreed to meet at his parents' penthouse in Jacksonville on the Intercoastal Waterway. That launched the next step in determining possible sailing mates. I needed to know sailing destinations and how safe the boat and competent the captain and most important, the nature or personality of the captain. Only one woman answered my ad. She was putting together a racing team.

My first interview, which was with Paul, was a fiasco. Well educated, well healed, he seemed acceptable at first. The conversation at lunch killed the deal for me. As a powerful executive at a large corporation across the state line, he spoke not so much of products, but who his workers were and how difficult he found the management of women. They wanted wages equal to those of men. They got pregnant. They had children. And they were always pressuring the company to provide child day care while they worked. They were totally unreasonable, he said, and I quickly judged him the same. We actually shouted at each other in that restaurant.

Another early failed interview was on Amelia Island with a big-bellied, gray-bearded captain about fifty-five and his forty-year-old woman. She wore a multi-colored head scarf and skirts to the floor, not exactly appropriate gear to climb ladders or address boat repairs. Their unkempt boat was *on the hard*, meaning it was stored in a boatyard on wooden cradles. To get into the boat, I climbed the ladder and was surprised to discover a pot-bellied stove burning wood, a rocking chair, and relics of the sixties. This pair played music at island clubs and seriously needed extra labor and organization if ever they were to sail. I could see they would not be ready to do so in at least a year, but then, they were in a world of their own. I stopped by to check on them after one of those horrible hurricanes and of course the boat was lying on its side on the ground, even more damaged.

Next, I drove to Asheboro, North Carolina, eagerly anticipating the successful stockbroker who had sent pictures of his golden retriever, his renovated historical house, boat, and dinghy. The house was to be shown in the Parade of Homes the next Sunday. Between what I saw of the perfectly restored dinghy and his beautifully decorated house with tapestries, rugs, sterling, and tasteful furniture, I knew I was following a superior craftsman, a gentle soul, and a never-married bachelor to his slip at the Oriental Marina. We agreed to take his forty-two-foot yacht on a try-out along the coast. How could this be better crafted? No way. My answer was "Yes, yes, this is it," as the transducer, aka the speedometer/knot meter showed quickly increasing speed. As the knot meter showed 12 knots, I realized that my captain was unaware that he did not have adequate control of the craft.

I asked, remembering that I was the guest, "What do you think about reefing the mainsail?"

This we promptly did. With me at the helm, his yacht heeling more than he could handle, he reefed his mainsail. On our return to the marina, I knew he was ready to travel the world with me, but I pretended that I had another interview and could not commit at this time. Two weeks later, he and his golden retriever were in my parents' backyard having tea.

"Sorry," I lied. "I have made other plans."

Three of the other near hits of the fifteen tryouts I conscientiously completed were of note because of their contrasting times in the captains' lives. The forty-two-year-old retired Navy electrical engineer purchased and refurbished a used boat. He wanted to live aboard in the Keys. Having spent his life at sea, he demonstrated confidence, a clear plan, and had an open invitation to find safe harbor at any navy port. We ate in the officers' dining rooms and sometimes had access to the PX. We got along, did our jobs, and arrived at Marathon on the way to Key West. After about a week of togetherness, I decided this match would not fly because we never had great conversations, I was not interested in him sexually, and he had yet to plan a serious distant destination.

The second fellow of note had been abandoned by his wife. She had had enough of a hard lifestyle and returned to land, leaving him with lace curtains covering the portholes and antimacassars (essentially lace doilies) on the lounge. I believed he would be depressed for a long time although he did put up a tough front.

Finally, again before cell phones, I was traveling south from New York and returned a call to an Amway salesman with a beautiful forty-foot craft. The man, who was looking for a sailing companion, was driving south on the east coast of North Carolina on HWY 95. I was within a hundred miles of the same road, and we agreed to meet at the southeast corner of an unknown intersection between 95 and a highway, not in a town. By selecting an approximate time, we agreed to go to a diner if one were visible. Otherwise, we were to wait at the planned rendezvous time for an hour.

This actually worked. Soon after arriving in Ft. Lauderdale, I began preparing his boat for a test sail when I realized the man's son, who had just graduated from college, was not eager to share time with his father and an unknown woman. I understood the issue and returned to my parents' home.

Another option, this time with an owner of several banks and a board member of the Broward County Council of Cultural Affairs, had me dining at the Boca Raton Yacht Club. I wore a demure pink suit; he wore khakis, deck shoes without socks, a T-shirt, and a dinner jacket. His mansion felt like a mausoleum on one of those many inlets in Boca. Both architecture and furnishings revealed a Bauhaus influence. As his maid made up my bed elsewhere in this grand house, he continued unrelentingly to interview me. What a role reversal.

A week later, he paid for my airfare to fly to Eleuthera. Picking me up at the airport, he jumped out of his jeep, opened my door, and presented me with roses. Shortly, we arrived by tender to his yacht, and he introduced me to his thirty-five-year-old captain and explained that the young man, the son of a surgeon, preferred to sail rather than graduate from Harvard.

As expected and of special interest to me, was the sixty-two-foot, brand new, winged keel work of art. I had never been on a sailboat this well-equipped and beautiful. The bank president and his captain wanted a party, so the next day, the owner left the mooring to gather up a few young women. Two came, clad in bikinis, glad for the invitation, agenda undisclosed. As the evening ticked on, they drank, a lot, and ultimately went to bed with the captain.

I already had a strong sense of the agenda, which he had not presented to me in Boca Raton. The owner wanted an intelligent hostess, manager of housekeeping and food, and a willing lover. Despite the beauty of the yacht, this demeaning reality was a complete turn off and deal-killer. Fortunately, I had already moved into my single room as the partying conversation turned to anticipating race week. This International Regatta and associated racing is reputedly the crown jewel of Caribbean racing and draws what I would label many of the "biggy bigs" in my classifications of men or yachts. I could hear the owner and captain lasciviously recalling last year's assembly, laughingly naming which yachts had the most breasts hanging over the lifelines. Understanding the agenda and having no problem with it, these young women, barely out of their teens, were ripe for the picking. They removed their bras to show their goods and laughed. My decision to leave as soon as possible was definitely confirmed. We flew back to the mainland and just before parting I asked him, "What are your plans for the day?"

His answer. "Buy another bank."

Chapter Eight

Ari went by only that one name and felt anything else a redundancy. He had responded to my ad in *Cruising World*, so I arranged to meet this stranger at the Hilton Hotel on the Tampa Bay.

I introduced myself to him, and when he answered with his first name, I asked, "Ari who?"

"Just Ari," he said, and gave me a look that said it was time to change the subject.

Yet, he was the ticket to my goal, and if I could make this work, I wanted it. From the way he avoided the restaurant, I thought he must have no money for coffee, so I looked for an unused room in which we could talk. The ballroom was empty, and there we stood with floor-to-ceiling, partially drawn brocade curtains stingily letting in late afternoon light. There were neither couches nor chairs. *How do I begin?* Extremely tense, I conspicuously stood in the center of the luxurious ballroom, face to face with a stranger whose German accent reminded me of my grandparents. He looked like a relative. He sounded like a relative. However, he was by no means a relative. I continued thinking *How do I get this interview started?*

Impulsively, I asked him to dance. Looking back, I realize I was sending a mixed message. At the time, it didn't occur to me. I was nervous, and although I wanted to relax the situation, sex was the last thing on my mind.

I think it was the last thing on his mind as well. However, he won points on my mental checklist for enjoying the spontaneity of the waltz as we hummed the melody of *The Blue Danube*. Then we talked. His mother, an MD, had paid for his schooling, and as an engineer, he had owned an electrical lighting design business. As a child after the war, he survived in Frankfurt, playing war games with other pre-teen boys, using sticks for guns and abandoned hand grenades, which added to their imagined excitement. The kids never knew if they were throwing duds at their friends or real weapons. When I visited Frankfurt years later, I imagined Ari playing among the still existing mounds of rubble and shells of majestic cathedrals. These areas remain today as reminders of WWII, for all who may care to reflect.

His wife had left him, taking her ten solid-gold bracelets to serve in the Buddhist Rajneeshee's colony of two thousand disciples in Oregon. Her position was high in the hierarchy. He said she was an accountant, traveling throughout the world with this renowned guru. The stories of his twenty-plus Rolls Royces must have been tallied in her records, and years later, all this came to light when the ashram crashed.

Ari had crossed the Atlantic at least eight times, probably more, but I fear exaggerations were part of his nature, and I never knew the real truth. He lived totally by barter. It was amazing to see how that worked here in the United States in Florida. His life was so different from anything I had known that I remained fascinated with his lessons regarding sailing, boat maintenance, his fabricated or real stories, and his constant plan to re-cross the Atlantic. On board, he quickly introduced me first to the food I would be cooking, and then other responsibilities in the galley. He ate only macrobiotic meals, which I had never heard of, and he introduced me to his dietary requirements regarding herbs and other organic foods, including freshly caught, fast swimming seafood. I learned to balance our meals representing Yin or acidic foods such as grains or nuts with Yang, which meant potatoes, beets, carrots, rutabagas, and any of the root vegetables. I learned to cook this way for six months.

Each evening, we would lay out oats, raisins, and grated carrots, bringing them to a boil, so that by morning, our breakfast was waiting. There was no ice, and if I let any of the greens rot in the Florida heat, he held me responsible. With his German accent and rigid thinking, his world was either "richtig" or "nicht in ordnung." The yelling reminded me of my dad's anger, and because I was clearly inured to my father's craziness, I also considered Ari's explosions just noise. I do admit I always remembered to keep my mouth shut, knowing who I was dealing with. Although I knew this life was temporary, I found it difficult to leave because he was so instructive. My payoff for accepting his craziness was an education I could never have learned in graduate school.

Semera, his yacht, was remarkable. The stained-glass windows made of triple-thickness glass could withstand the heaviest seas. As an engineer particularly proficient in metals, he designed the drawers to slide on stainless steel tracks and rollers. They always locked automatically, so that when foul weather occurred (again this is before Loran or SatNav warnings), the interior was always buttoned down, ready to take the storm.

The main salon did not have the typical drop-leaf table, but rather elaborate, deep seating, something like a sofa or lounge. The unusual design of the benches allowed passengers to sit with their backs against heavy skins called Flokati. These off-white wool skins purchased in the Greek Mountains while Ari was still sailing the Mediterranean were long haired, very comfortable, moisture resistant, and perfect for mealtime comfort.

We leaned against them with legs bent toward our faces and placed our plates on our knees. Should crumbs fall, we never noticed because they were lost in the long hair of sheep or goats. One of my early jobs was to take these heavy animal skins that were six-by-eight feet and drag them to an outside newly-rigged clothesline. He instructed me to beat them with "the banger," something like a broom, knocking out all those months of crumbs.

Then I washed them, enjoying the activity, the suds, the coolness of the water in the Florida heat, scrubbing hard with the hand brush. After they dried, I dragged them back to the boat, getting some needed help from the captain. In my thinking, this way of eating was a great improvement over the classic salon table because we had lots of space, and we could actually recline, enjoying the coziness of the furs and the stability of our positions. When possible, I still favor eating this way.

Ari introduced me to his friends, who called him Doc. They were his groupies and admired his experience at sea, his innovations, and his capacity with engines and motors. As I studied those people, I realized he was always manipulative enough to have friends who were rich and generous. They offered us an unoccupied marina slip at no extra fee or a bedroom in their luxurious homes whenever we visited.

In the background, there always seemed to be a clandestine business transaction of which I knew nothing. I was most suspicious of friends in Central Florida near Tampa, tall unshaven dirty-looking brutes, who must have had a history with Ari. I saw him negotiate long-term use of their VW in exchange for a total repair of the engine. This he did quickly. We arrived one morning to their small average ranch house and were invited to a breakfast consisting of huge, bloody steaks, which neither of us ate.

We were waited on by a tiny fragile-looking woman who could have been Twiggy of the 1960s. Her role was to be their housekeeper and probably their sex partner. What really put me on edge was just seeing the gun safe that took up half the living room.

This observation, along with spending a night at one of their friends' homes further raised my awareness that I was in another layer of society I had never known. He had his whole kitchen set up to make bullets, including vises, grinders, screwdrivers, and drill bits. This "friend" was the mildest of men, and I was hard-pressed to see the connection. Probably money, or perhaps politics.

Related to this ever-constant wariness, I recalled Ari's telling me about his time in Saudi Arabia. Again, traveling in a VW, he encountered a desert sandstorm during which the sand was gradually burying more and more of his car. He told me he was always afraid the Saudis would catch him. His assignment had been to make a quick desert crossing, traveling the one-lane, windblown back roads. The storm was unexpected, and he had no choice as he hunkered down to breathe and survive. Later, not knowing what his cargo had been, I suspected he was a gun runner there and in the states, after he disclosed his secret storage caches on *Semera*. He never showed me exactly where they were but said they were integrated into the mosaic of artistic and complicated pattern of the interior wood. That's all he revealed. I continued to live either a real or imagined life of mystery. Because of living with Ari, I believe secrets are ever present in most of our lives.

Ari had connections in Brandon, where he stayed some of the time, and also in Tampa. *Semera* was tied up to a dock offered to Ari by German friends in La Belle, east of

Ft. Myers. This fed into the Inter Coastal Waterway, allowing passage east to the Atlantic. We traversed Lake Okee-
chobee to find there was no place to tie up for the night.
Anchoring would have placed us mid-channel, and because
we desired no unexpected encounter with tugboat-pushing
barges, we allowed ourselves to tie up to insecure pilings
rather than power through the night.

We knew we would quickly be in trouble if the pilings
gave way, but we went with the odds, knowing there was
little traffic at this time of the day, and the worst that could
happen was external damage. The next day, we motored the
last half of the ditch, otherwise known as the dugout, a constructed waterway east to west or west to east, depending
on which friends we were going to meet. This is a very boring passage with nothing to see but the walls of the ditch, a
few seabirds, and grasses. The engine pulsed incessantly at
a steady 5 knots. Progress was slow. I was bored and hot
and lethargic. We encountered no other travelers other than
some small power boats until we were well into the intercoastal waterway. However, I was increasingly alert to
Ari's increasing wariness.

"When you're at the helm, I want you to be extra
observant of incoming or following traffic," he said, "so I
may clearly identify them before they get too close."

This "identifying" appeared to me a little over the top,
but then what did I know? He had told me about the sail
loft fire he had been falsely accused of setting. I had heard
of his good fortune in finding "abandoned" supplies, including rolls of Dacron he claimed had fallen off the truck.
His friends seemed accepting of every excuse and every
story, and I was in no position to challenge him, and I was
left with the option to leave or to learn more of Ari's alternate reality.

When a vessel approached and was close, I noted that
he physically reduced his visibility, kept his hat low, sun-

glasses secure, and often asked me to take the helm. As we joined the heavy boating traffic between Palm Beach and South Miami, the U.S. Coast Guard became increasingly visible. They could legally board us with the slightest provocation. Ari's paranoia increased. That's when I learned that he did not have a legal passport or boat registration. Because I had moved my car to the area, he asked me to mail an envelope to Texas. Weeks later, a letter with a Texas return address arrived at a friend's home. I surmised it contained a passport.

Several of his riveting stories qualified him for long-term imprisonment, but then, I never knew which, if any, of the stories were true. I had never actually witnessed criminal activity.

Perhaps he told me these stories to entertain me, much as if offering to share the story of a novel or a film. One such story was adapted to film by Herzog, an international filmmaker. Herzog, in his own madness, determined to make a film based on a story set in the Peruvian rainforest. His protagonist, the lunatic dreamer Fitzcarraldo, acted by Klaus Kinski, intended to portage his 320-ton steamship over a hill five hundred miles north of the nearest city to access rubber. The setting of an isolated, impossible environment would contrast with the main character's passion to access wealth by harvesting rubber and then create a functioning opera house five hundred miles north of the nearest major city. The hero taught actors and native laborers how to use a block and tackle system to bring the supplies and talent needed to build the opera house. To add to the insanity of the situation, Caruso recordings played as the laborers worked until the needle of the recorder broke. Everyone was vulnerable to disease, dysentery, snakes, tarantulas, loss of limb, and death. Some abandoned the project.

Ari gave me a remarkable gift in telling me about the

film, which I later saw as an important exploration of dreams, reality, creativity and being. During the making of the film, Herzog became Fitzcarraldo, never acknowledgeing he was living the hero's life. He was in the moment, aware of the danger. He accepted this as his life, his reality for that time. Like the filmmaker and the actor, I do not wish to abandon what is, but to live fully and see what there is as I accept the challenge of the mountain and then look beyond.

Another of Ari's stories was about a women shipmate. He returned to *Semera* one night to find her secretly using his short-wave radio. He quietly told me, "I beat her, probably broke her leg, and she was off the boat by morning." He said he believed she was a spy.

Truth or fiction? I will never know, but as we spent months together, I was always careful to avoid breaking his rules. Yes, by now, I knew what it was like to live with a psychopath. I asked myself: *How many psychologists get beyond textbooks, office visits, and court evaluations?* The answer didn't matter. I was absorbed with my life, I was living aboard, and I was now acquainted with layers of society I would never have even read about. I was ever hopeful of sailing the Atlantic. All our work supported that goal, and I looked forward to meeting his friends who lived along the Mediterranean.

One friend of Ari's we visited was a surgeon who had developed cervical cryosurgery as a method to treat cancer. He made a good penny because he was much in demand. His dining table was replete with Baccarat Crystal, and of course, we enjoyed yet another high-rise view of the ocean. What was especially curious to me was the MD's seventeen-year-old daughter, who flirted outrageously with Ari. He went to bed with her that night. It didn't matter to me. We were not sexual, and I was happy to have the bed to myself.

Another field trip was a visit to the inventor of a newly designed auto helm, a steering mechanism that alleviates total vigilance at the helm on long-distance runs. He put us up at his condo on a Miami inlet, and we later joined him free of charge at the Miami Boat Show, where he was demonstrating and selling his newly designed product, an improvement over past models. At mealtime, when we wanted to share our healthy food, that highly credentialed captain laughed and said, "Thank you, but no thank you."

That particular meal consisted of donkey rolls, an Ari original made from large seaweed leaves filled with beans and rice, grated carrots, flavored with tamari and daikon radish.

An innocent in Ari's collection of "friends" was a very young man who owned a shoe factory that employed Guatemalans. Of course, he supplied Ari with free deck shoes. I do not know what Ari gave him, possibly access to Ari's continuing group of admirers.

One extraordinary experience was one I took on as I said, "No way this is going to happen." My assignment was get *Semera* fitted with free solar panels. The plan was to call a manufacturer and tell him I wanted to learn about his operation and products. He was only too pleased to have me come to his plant because he thought I was a freelance writer for boating magazines. I did not counter this misunderstanding. I was impressed with the varieties of solar panels and how they functioned in the military as well in the yachting world. At the end of the visit, which I truly enjoyed, I brought back to *Semera* two brand new flexible solar panels, which provided electricity when shore power was not available. A generator was expensive to run. Panels had no cost.

The 98-degree day I parted company with Ari occurred when we were *on the hard*. The boat had been lifted out of the water and carried by a huge crane to a cradle, so that we

could access the hull, scrape barnacles, drill into the os-
motic, foul-smelling bubbles in the fiber-glass, and prep the
yacht for repairs. We filled the holes with fiber cloth and
fiberglass. The hull being freshly sanded was ready for two
coats of bottom paint. My real agenda for putting up with
Ari was to learn and to experience things inaccessible to me
in any other way. Even these chores, difficult as they may
be, were exciting. How does a Ph.D. psychologist get to
work like a boatyard hand?

As he was sanding the hull, I was in the galley preparing lunch. Macrobiotic meals do not allow for easy sandwiches, and most are made of fresh foods.

Working in the boatyard, we were miserable without
AC. Most yachts did have it. Unfortunately we did not.
However, that was no excuse for Ari's explosive behavior.
Frustrated with his task, he swore, he screamed, he threw
his stainless steel water cup high into the air. Speeding first
upward, above the dodger and then downward into the
galley, the cup whizzed by my head like a baseball, and I
knew I'd had enough.

It was a big decision to give up all that work anticipating an Atlantic crossing, but I would not risk it. I turned off
the stove, left the food on the counter, hurriedly gathered
up my clothing, put it into my dry sack, climbed down the
ladder, and once I was safely out of reach, said, "I'm leaving."

No arguments. No discussions. I no longer felt safe. As
quickly as we had joined our lives, we parted. I wasn't
about to do a crossing with someone capable of random
violence,

Throughout the six months we shared, I knew Ari was
a con. I never saw him commit a crime, but I knew he was
always potentially dangerous. He provided me free room
and board, interesting company, healthy eating, and lessons
in sailboat maintenance and navigation. I gave him free

labor, attention, and two solar panels. It was an extra-ordinary course of study I could never have purchased in departments of psychology or maritime studies. I had chosen to live, to learn, and to leave a conflicted, potentially dangerous man.

About one month later, I was talking to a highly credentialed captain I met through Ari and asked, "What's Ari doing these days? Has he left for Europe?"

"Not yet," the captain answered. "He's training his new first mate, a woman from Manhattan who deals in the buying and selling of baseball cards. She's paying him six hundred dollars a month in order to replace your position." I thought *Good luck. May she survive without harm.*

ANITA VLISMAS

Chapter Nine

Disappointed I had not yet achieved a blue-water crossing, I reviewed my efforts, which had totally failed in identifying an appropriate ship and captain. But then, still unexplored inquiries waited for my consideration.

I define blue-water sailing as being long-term, self-sufficient, and able to cope in every situation for more than two days. If I found the right vessel, I would be out there for weeks, unable to see the shoreline, which immediately makes many sailors wary. In contrast, offshore sailing is much more predictable because within twenty-four hours, you have a better sense of the weather than predicting a week into the future.

Offshore sailing also creates a feeling of security because we like to think we can always reach the shoreline if something goes wrong. Blue-water creates a bigger challenge for the captains. You can't just put the bow of the boat in the direction you want to head. The currents may be pushing you elsewhere, and the elements need to be included in the navigational plan. Should you sail far enough off shore, there are currents and tides that are less affected by the mainland and respond to the influence of the continents between oceans. These change by the season, but they are consistent.

It's about understanding the technology of the international currents and gravitational pulls of sea and land. A lot of things are happening on the planet. A good captain does his or her best to know what they are at any given time. You can't just point your boat at a certain longitude and latitude. I was looking for a captain who could do that and also someone who could use the sextant I brought in case he didn't have his own. All equipment eventually breaks, and I needed someone who could navigate by the stars in addition to the chart plotter. Of course I never saw a GPS, a computerized global positioning system, although I heard they were being developed.

That eight-inch pile of inquiries was still stacked under my bed in my parents' guest room. Soon, I was talking to Daryl, an Alaskan, who as an Indiana high school graduate, had decided his future was in creating a power plant in Beetles, Alaska. Initially, he did not have a lot of money. Using a sledge and massive trucks to move equipment across the wilderness of northern Canada and Alaska, he had to time the arrival of materials for building this plant between impossible snow, mud, and sodden spring rains. With focus and ambition, his dream successfully brought electricity to a town that previously had none, and he was free to sail his dreams.

Talking long distance from Hawaii, Daryl had very much impressed me as he shared his history and told me he was changing crew. He wanted me to fly to New Zealand to replace two who would return to the states. I would be an adequate first mate if we were correct in our initial, over-the-phone, assessments. He would pay for a round-trip ticket, guaranteeing my safe return if I was not satisfied with him or his craft. He had already sailed from Alaska to California and then to Hawaii. His plans were for me to be the only crew for the expected two-week voyage to Australia. I was to cook and be alert and on watch every six hours.

When we met, he took me to a smorgasbord near Auckland, where I ate my first kiwis, passion fruit, papayas, and to me, rare and wonderfully prepared foods. His boat, my first steel-hulled craft, had just been repainted red, had no headliner, and was in good condition given its thorough yet barebones equipment. He was a gentleman, showing patience as he answered what to him may have been naive questions. "What will you do if the navigations equipment breaks down? Why do you not have a headliner?" On a side trip by ferry, across the Bay of Isles to Russell, which is reputedly the sailfish and marlin fishing capital of the world, I remained relaxed and thoroughly enjoyed the abundance of flower gardens bordering small cottages.

The crossing (departing Auckland located in northeastern New Zealand, heading north toward Norfolk Island, and then east to Brisbane) was to take around fourteen days. I had a smile on my face as I took the helm and Daryl lifted anchor. Subsequently, 30- to 45-knot head winds buffeted us fourteen of eighteen days. I easily lost ten pounds by way of puking.

Wind buried our voices and burned our faces. We wore foul-weather gear on deck and inside. Despite painful retching, I kept my watches, eyes barely open, yet definitely open to guard against any random cargo ships, a constant lethal threat. Not all cargo ships had functioning radar, and often, they could not see us. If they did, it took eons to change their course. It was up to us to stay out of the way.

I never regretted my choice to take this voyage until, totally depleted from my only major experience with sea sickness, I begged to be put in at Norfolk Island.

Daryl said, "No. Impossibly dangerous. Too many rocky cliffs."

So that was that, and I continued to puke. Obviously, cooking was difficult. First, it's no fun when the cook was nauseated. Second, the stove could not be locked down, meaning the fire was not exactly stable. When the only frying pan, cast iron with a fifteen-inch diameter, flew out of the oven, I screamed. It missed me and hit the wall with a fatal crack. Not me. Not the wall. Only the fifteen-inch frying pan was damaged. Without a replacement, I cooked with a leaking frying pan for another week. Those gray, stormy days with frequent thirty-foot seas, forced us to grab whatever bracing came to hand. Waves banging on the hull actually pained my body. Howling headwinds deadened any daydreaming. The unrelenting nausea abated only with the sighting of the Brisbane shoreline, still miles away. The wave action quieted. We dropped the tender.

Of course, I would never share the fact that there were a few hours when I regretted taking this passage. *Would I do this again?* My quick answer will always be an unequivocal *Yes.* I was totally focused on doing whatever was necessary to survive. I was fully alive, alert, using both strength and mind to participate fully in life in the moment. I felt my "nothingness." I was ultimately alone in the world, and at the same time, I was part of the whole. The noise of wind, the unpredictability of the sea, the movement of the boat encapsulated me. I was intensely aware of my being part of the ALL.

As the seas calmed, normalcy returned, and we arrived on a Brisbane shore. I now had access to a bigger, broader experience. We landed our tender at a boatyard that stored cargo containers, each one glorifying all the brilliant colors I learned as a child. Red. Blue. Green. Yellow. Orange. Walking among these minor monoliths, I was humble and grateful and almost vibrating to the intensity of color. In contrast to the sea, color had become absolutely thrilling. Together, we relocated to a proper marina and thoroughly enjoyed the amenities of a hot shower, a Vegemite sandwich, and a gently rocking berth.

Now the question was, "What next?"

Daryl had to return to Beetles to check on his business, and I agreed to attend to his boat, turning the engine on once a week, cleaning the decks, checking the lines. On his return, we planned to rent a car and tour the east coast of Australia.

After he left, I discovered I was free to visit the yacht club, buy a bike and fresh food, shop flea markets, do my laundry, take the train to the city center, dance in the public square, and finally rent a car. The bike was my first ticket to initially explore Australia, a country about which I knew little. Actually, I had never even thought about either New Zealand or Australia as destinations. I'd had no interest. But here I was, aware there is always something to learn, and I love an open slate.

First, I considered whether I could find work. I visited the University of Queensland and met the chairman of the Psychology Department. She informed me Australia did not need more doctors, but definitely more panel beaters and plumbers. I inquired about bartending. Lack of experience cancelled that option. I talked about bean picking, one of the hardest, most difficult jobs entailing hours of squatting and sore hands. Oh well, a segue onto other things followed my feeble attempts to work.

I bought a well-used bike from the Australian Poste that would make it easier to get to the city-bound train. I bought a three-quarter-length, long-sleeved, red gauze dress with nickel-sized polka dots, and put my curly brown hair into a dramatic braid. I was definitely ready to see the city and for the city to see me. The locals informed me Brisbane had public dancing in the square at noon and free organ recitals in the city-center church.

On my first outing, I met a man on the train who was returning to his family after a day's work. We talked a bit, and I thought he understood I would be happy to meet his family, including his children, and he could contact me through the Manley Marina. Three nights later, when I had already settled into the beginnings of sleep, I heard a man calling, "Anita," his voice loud and clear.

There, without the light of a moon, I could see him skulling a "borrowed" dinghy at my stern. Somehow, he came to the marina, untied somebody's dinghy, and arrived at my boat.

"There must have been a misunderstanding," I called. "I never intended we would meet privately." I did not hear from him again.

On another outing to the city center, I met an enthusiastic Scotsman, who eagerly shared his knowledge of the area. Because of his classic brogue, most of what he said I could not understand, but his intentions were good. I was happy to learn about the yacht club one-half kilometer (about one-quarter mile) south of my marina.

There, other adventures began. First, Corolla, a twenty-two-year-old, invited me to race with her against "the boys." To our amazement, we came in first. Forever after, they placed us under a handicap, as much because the Aussies could not tolerate being beaten by women, and also because Corolla's sixteen-foot boat was truly lighter and faster. It did warrant a handicap. Dancing after the races allowed me to meet a few single guys.

Usually, the lean, strong skippers were married to portly wives, who were also enjoying a night out in the club's dining area. They gossiped, drank richly creamed coffee, and ate scones served with clotted cream and fruit. They also knitted absolutely gorgeous wool or cotton sweaters, and, ever the art appreciator, I ordered gift sweaters made of wool because I thought cotton was not worthy of their craftsmanship.

After the second race, I again danced with one of the younger men I had met earlier and still fancied. Fifteen minutes later, we were leaving for my boat only to have me abruptly stop in the parking lot and exclaim, "I can't just leave my bike here."

With the savoir-faire of French royalty, this skinny boat carpenter extended his arm, grabbed my bike with one hand, and swooped it into the bed of his truck, never letting go of my arm. With me, the bike and truck, we arrived at my berth, and we continued to enjoy the night.

Increasing confidence with Australian rules of the road fostered my courage to explore north and slightly western Queensland, again not too far. Australia is as big as the United States without the population. That translated to traveling relatively long destinations with unexpected access to extremely rural towns with no visible stores, one bar, and rarely a park with rangers or plumbing or even hikers. The billabongs, fresh water pools, amphibians, and lotus flowers drew emus that raced me from a distance on my western route.

Not counting on human visibility, let alone help, I relied on my well-traveled car, maps, water (enough for forty-eight hours), and a hope that there would be help should I need it. In addition to the water, I carried a supply of salami, tinned tuna, hard cheese, bread, fruit, carrots, and a bedroll. Soil differences were sometimes extreme, mostly when miles of red dust kicked up. Unexpected sightings of the abundance of emus and ostriches running thirty miles an hour or koala bears hidden in their eucalyptus trees sleepily munching, kept me in a child's world of discovery. Unrecognizable trees I later identified as Paper Bark, more than ninety-feet tall, or Moreton Bay Figs, known in the states as Banyan Trees, distinctively paraded roots one to two feet wide growing upward from the base or hanging down from the arbor.

Driving late afternoon while traveling a country road through miles and miles of open range, I hoped a sleeping place would magically present comfort and food. And voila, a two-story ranch house appeared—not a mirage, but close. About ten ranch hands were ending their workday with beer and camaraderie around the dartboard and pool table of what was actually referred to as hotel. The bartender told me there were no sleeping quarters available. He said the two rental bedrooms upstairs were being painted and totally unfit for a guest.

Self-conscious with considerable fatigue, I let a few tears drop and asked if it was possible for me to have a spot behind his sofa in his family's part of the building. He spoke with his wife, who kindly offered to share their family dinner, and opened one of the unfinished rooms, moving the cans, brushes, and ladders. I was careful not to mess up the new paint. The parents and four children dined with me, eager to have an American all to themselves. They taught me that port wine is the classy way to end dinner with a guest, sharing their stories as they showed me genuine warmth and acceptance.

The next morning, we again met for breakfast and began discussing college opportunities in the states for the children. We stayed in contact for five years, and I returned to visit a year later. Not much had changed. The upstairs needed repainting again because the dry winds always left a film of grunge.

Another evening, driving without a plan, I again anticipated a difficult night because the land was without trees or houses. Fortunately, I spotted an inconsequential house beside a private lake. With calm courage, if such a quality exists, I stopped the car near the house. There was no driveway. Then I walked to the door, knocked, and asked the man who answered it, "Can I park overnight near your lake?"

He generously agreed.

The lake was a quarter-mile from his house, and I slept in my bedroll, basically a light blanket and small pillow. No luxury of a tent in those days. I was extremely careful not to leave waste. As the sun quickly set, and I gratefully crawled under the quilt, thankful it was too hot for mosquitoes, I heard the most frightful, unidentifiable sound: Not a bark, not a growl, not a scream, not a cackle, not a croak. *Perhaps it's one of those wild dingoes who run off with children. What's the smartest thing to do? Wrap the blanket tightly so critters cannot get vulnerable me. Cover your head.* My noisy heart calmed. I slept.

The next morning, arriving at a tourist destination in the Glass House Mountains, I heard that same, awful, frightening sound emerging from bushes. Images of wild creatures I had seen in my travel books about Australia increased my caution, but I had to know. With my heart beating above my normal seventy beats a minute, yet ever the adventurer, I cautiously walked into that undergrowth and was shocked to meet a ten-year-old youngster who was practicing his kookaburra imitations, a sound I will always remember. Laughing kookaburras, part of the kingfisher family, are indigenous only to northeastern Australia and New Guinea.

By this time, I truly was missing "the news" and the music of radio. My car had neither. However, still not ready to return to the boat, I found myself driving on a first class National Park country road with one and a half lanes paved. I was enjoying the contrast of rich, moist greenery.

Unexpectedly, my old warrior model of a car choked and croaked. I knew this would have to happen at some point in my travels. Normally, I would simply flag down another vehicle. However, there were no cars. I waited, fifteen, thirty, sixty minutes and then decided I would have to walk for help. Being fit and relying on a map, actually a placemat, I anticipated a town some distance down my road. I walked through the drizzle, loving the variegated green grasses, enjoying the frogs, salamanders, and a few small snakes that immediately slithered away. No problem, really.

I heard the truck before it was visible. Passing my car clearly stopped by the side of the road a few miles back, the driver knew I obviously needed help. He stopped, gave me a lift to the town and the laundromat, setting a priority of drying my clothes. Maybe he knew something I did not. He took my car keys and passed them on to the owner of the service station, a friend of his. In these places, it appears everyone is a friend, and of course, happy for business. The mechanic would find me at the laundromat after he assessed my situation with the car. My good Samaritan continued with his day's work.

I agreed I needed to get dry. The laundromat, devoid of customers, was an obvious place to begin, but how? Dry clothes were in the car—somewhere. Everything I was wearing was thoroughly soaked. I was shivering with cold. There was not a store to sell me new, dry clothes, and I did not have the money for them anyway. Self-consciously, awkwardly, feeling outrageously conspicuous, I stripped to my undies, and immediately became lightheaded. My bare legs, my arms, my midriff were smeared with blood. My clothes looked like bloody rags as they patterned the white tiled floor. Quick to react and not knowing leeches should not be pulled off as their head might remain under the skin, I systematically began to pull on each of those one to three-inch bloodsucking parasites.

If I wanted an exciting, informative life experience, here it was. My car was broken down in a wilderness, and I was alone, cold and wet with leeches sucking my blood.

My only prior experience with leeches was through novels set in the seventeenth century when the physician was using them to save the hero's life. As I pulled them off, my blood flowed harder. Disgusted, I threw all the clothes into the washer. The leeches went into the trash. I went into the washroom and cleaned up, using cold water. There were no paper towels. The floors could not be wiped. As I sat waiting for my gear to dry, I was aware of my shivering, but what's the thing to do? This was a different kind of life, albeit a bit uncomfortable. No real damage. And I was engaged fully.

Later, the mechanic told me the news about the car. I was fortunate. I had to stay only one extra night. That was enough. I finally decided to return to Daryl's boat in Brisbane.

ANITA VLISMAS

Chapter Ten

I had no other agenda at the moment, and I might have continued this way, enjoying Brisbane and the gentle rocking of the sailboat. I was aware that my driven personality temporarily had no specific focus. I was just in a comfortable state of being as I explored maps of the countryside and notices about local activities. However, unknown to me, a thirty-five-year-old "retired" electrical engineer had been watching me through binoculars as I washed clothes on the dock in my red bikini.

One afternoon, after a day in town, I was riding my bike on the dock, returning to my boat. There he was approaching with a sombrero and impenetrable sunnies. I stopped in front of the sombrero and sunglass-wearing stranger because riding the bike and passing him on that narrow dock was asking for trouble.

Within six weeks, we were married.

I'm getting ahead of myself, so let me back up to that first moment on the dock. Because of his garb, he radiated mystery. Consistent with who I am, I wanted to know more about him as I fumbled for something friendly to say. In that moment school children were passing between us, and

I asked, "Do you like children?" Much later, he told me he understood this as, "Do you want to make babies with me?"

We continued to our boats, and shortly, he appeared at my stern (sailboats are usually backed in), and said, "I see you washing clothes and bed sheets on the dock. I have a car. Would you like me to drive you to the laundry?"

"Sure." Easy answer. Then a pause, and I added, "Oh, I've promised that tomorrow I'll assist in a boat delivery from Gladstone through The Rip. If your offer's still good, could we do it afterward?"

"Sure." He calmly walked away still not having revealed his face.

On my return, two days later, he was waiting at my boat.

"On second thought," he said, "how about a climb in the mountains and a swim in the surf?"

Thoughts seemed to bubble in this man even when he appeared to have nothing on his mind. What answer could I possibly give?

"Sounds great, but first, I need a shower." I could tell he had made a decision to know this American-accented woman who rode a bike in a white polka-dotted red dress and lived on a boat in his country.

"I'll pick you up in an hour."

There he stood, an hour later, with a brown-paper grocery sack.

"I've brought bread, salami, cheese, chips, two apples, and water," he said. "That should take care of us for a while."

Ah, natural caregiver, I thought.

As we were leaving, I quickly ran into the marina office and told the staff, "I'm going off with the captain of *Nyalan*. I don't know his name, but if he returns today or later without me, call the police." They smiled and noted the message.

South of the city, we first climbed a rather steep hiking trail. Each time he climbed over a major boulder, he turned, asking if I could use a hand. I very much appreciated the offer, especially because of how it contrasted to my hiking days with Gene, when every "man" was for himself. And the offer was definitely an offer, not an expectation that I could not manage.

We dined at the summit, a slightly exaggerated description of a steep hiking trail, and returned to the car in time to reach Rainbow Beach before sunset. My companion, whose name I now knew was Wayne Vlismas, told me that his Uncle George had loaned him the key to his multi-million dollar unit, on one of the world's greatest surfing beaches. I was duly impressed although I never did get the hang of surf boarding.

We bought food to prepare for supper. Without discussion, we cooked together, cleaned up the galley, and retired early to our respective bedrooms as if we were an old married couple. However, the next morning, as we sat on the sofa drinking strong coffee and enjoying the breezes coming in from the east, I realized that this gentleman was not about to make "the move." For a moment, I considered my options.

This guy seems to be on the same page in life that I am. He wants to live aboard, not work only to pay taxes on a lifestyle he no longer values. He wants to sail long distances. He is strong, gentle, kind, technically competent, retired, single, looking for a mate—and he likes me. All right then. Do something.

I took a breath and somewhat awkwardly asked, "Would you like to kiss?"

We did. And we continued to share one bed until he died eighteen years later.

Within the week, Wayne took me to meet his family. We brought them bakery items and fruit, another reflection on Wayne's consideration for others and his love of good eating.

During a private conversation with his dad, I asked, "What do think of a serious match between your son and me? You should know he is fifteen years younger, and without family support, these things do not usually work out."

"If you'll have him, take him," his father said. "We thought he would never fall in love." So, with that parental blessing, we went forth.

Wayne had recently retired from major electrical engineering management responsibilities at an enormous petro chemical corporation that covered acres of land in Sydney. He had sold his condo, bought the boat in Brisbane, and moved on board, anticipating a life without property or income taxes. A lifelong sailor, he had the mind for navigation and mechanical tasks as well.

Wayne had never been engaged, let alone married, but shortly after I met his parents, he asked, "What do you think about marriage? Your visa will not allow you to remain here indefinitely."

I knew, as a single woman, I would have to return to work eventually, but as a married couple, we could pool our savings, take our time, and do what we wanted to do. *Marriage? Was I actually considering it? Yes, but first there were questions of where and when.*

Having eloped the first time, thirty-one years earlier, I had promised my very disappointed mother I would invite her to a second ceremony, should there ever be one. This meant we would go to the states, engage a cousin as the justice of the peace, and have a quiet family gathering. Neither of us put much value on ceremonies. However, my sixteen-years-younger brother, one year younger than Wayne, made an urgent call, asking if we could have a double wedding because his significant other was pregnant.

"No problem," I said.

Within days, fifty friends and family had been invited from New York, California, Tennessee, Ohio, Missouri, as well as Mexico and Australia. The caterers we interviewed were ignorant of the dishes Wayne wanted to serve our guests, so he directed our out-of-town guests and local neighbors to serve as sous chefs. He managed the menu. They peeled potatoes, made the casseroles, and placed flowers around the pool. The neighbors provided extra refrigerator space for the prepared dishes. The brides wrote the vows, and the poor grooms could do nothing but laugh as they attempted to cut the excess verbiage of two extremely verbal women who wanted to control for every contingency.

The grooms' biggest complaint was "Where's our bachelor party? We feel cheated." So, on the eve of the weddings, my sister offered to provide one. She gathered us into the hot tub, the brides, the grooms, and her husband as she presided. Nephews were the waiters immediately topping up anything we were drinking. Mom enjoyed the show, quietly watching as she sat on a lounge chair.

Wayne asked, "So, where's the action?"

"Watch," Laureen said.

She stripped off her bathing suit top and wiggled a bit as her husband climbed a King Palm tree. Our never-married man did not complain.

The next morning, Wayne and I were married. My father, demented because of Parkinson's disease, sat in his wheelchair, knowing his very important job was to give the bride away. For hours he repeatedly called out "I do. I do." I definitely was no longer his responsibility and chuckled throughout the day about his enthusiasm. At the same time, I was absolutely miserable with an extremely painful headache the entire day. As usual, I toughed it out, smiling and telling no one. After the meal and around nine that night, I said I was tired and went to my room to suffer alone. Excedrin was not helping. My sons opened my door around eleven o'clock that night.

"Mom, you've been in pain all day," Aaron said in a firm tone. "We're taking you to the emergency room."

"This can't go on." Kurt agreed.

Too feeble to argue, I let them take over. Wayne, Aaron, Kurt, and Aaron's wife, Diane, drove me to the ER, where I was treated and diagnosed for the first time at age fifty with migraines. I suffered these migraines since age thirty-five, keeping the degree of the pain to myself. It was bad enough having to admit to cancer, let alone chronic migraines. I considered pain in one form or another as part of living. At any moment, I can find pain in my body if I choose to, but I'm not interested in wasting my life focusing on what I cannot change.

Months earlier, I had unsuccessfully tried the most recent treatment protocols I researched in the hospital library. I tried remedies including dietary changes that failed as did the much-touted meditation and relaxation therapies. Going to the emergency room was not something I had considered until the night of my wedding. Demerol knocked me out. The next morning, I returned to my happy perspective on life and living well.

Our guests had finished the cleanup, and most of the wedding party had headed back home. Wayne's brother, our best man and a full participant at the hot tub bachelor party, and a couple of cousins joined us in a canoeing honeymoon.

Disappointment and shock streamed from my wet face following my abrupt discovery that Wayne did not know how to canoe. In front of everyone, my hero, who knew everything about the ocean dumped me. Totally wet, standing in waist-high water, I scolded, "How can you possibly not know how to canoe?"

That night, I gave him a reference book. Holding his own, he refused to read it. He did things on his own terms, and although often frustrated, I could not dominate him. I loved him for holding onto his independence. Over time, he eventually developed canoeing skills—when he was ready. I had learned that day my new husband would never be bullied.

Later that week, the stress of managing our wedding, being involved with silly family conflicts about who sits where or who books into which motels, had worn us down and caught us off guard. Driving in a part of the state I did not know, the two of us found ourselves arguing over something obviously minor.

"Stop the car," he demanded. "Let me out. I'm going to buy some cigarettes." This was his form of leveraging.

"You don't smoke."

"I used to," he said. "Stop the car. I will smoke if I want to."

As he was opening his door, I stopped, saying "If you go into that drugstore, I will not be here when you return."

He walked toward the store, and I furiously sped away only to realize, after calming down fifteen minutes later, I had no idea where I was or, more important, where he was. I had lost my husband in Florida.

Two and a half hours later, I finally found him sitting on the curb. He had not bought the cigarettes, still committed to being who he said he was. Having literally lost my new husband, I again learned something about stand-offs. Nobody wins. However, he did get the message that, for me, smoking was a deal breaker.

A week later, we returned to Manley Marina, Australia and began to plan our pleasures. I told Wayne about my agreement with Daryl Morris to rent a car and travel upon his return. I knew the two of them would get along. Their values were similar, choosing work that was not just for income and choosing the sea as a means to freedom.

"No problem," Wayne said. "We'll take him along in our car."

This we did, sharing the driving, the costs of camp-grounds, and four-bed cabins. Three beds were never available. Australian camping was especially luxurious compared to my earlier US car camping. We had money for rich barramundi sandwiches and pizza, usually with pineapple. We weren't drinkers, so there was another savings. As I saw the men become friends, I could hear Daryl trying to convince Wayne to be his crew for his return to Hawaii. Tempted, but fortunately preferring time with me, Wayne gave it a miss. But if he had chosen that passage, I would have managed until his return. He would have been great crew for Daryl because he knew what he was doing and never got sick during stormy seas. Daryl departed and later, when we were checking in on him, we learned he had married a sail maker

Wayne and I were now free without commitments. Our goal was to enjoy our lives while living within our means, and to avoid buying things that would not increase the quality of our lives. My car was literally gathering moss in my brother's backyard in California, and Wayne's remained in good form near Manley Harbor. Later, we gave up the Holden and relied only on my Honda CRV. The cars offered freedom to access places in Australia and later the United States or Canada. *Nyalan*, Wayne's sailboat, was more than adequate to travel from Melbourne to Cape York should we decide to sail those distances. We planned to live on his twenty-eight-foot boat our first year and sail wherever our inclinations took us. Later, in the states, we expected to buy a larger craft to continue world explorations.

The entire Australian continent beckoned. We were ready to explore and most important, we had time.

Anticipating camping in Australia, we had returned

from the states with my duffel bag filled to its maximum carrying weight of seventy pounds. The bag, stuffed with previously purchased quality camping equipment, including tent, mattresses, the classical Australian billy cooking pot, and silk sheets to keep out tiny critters, would enhance a comfortable and independent lifestyle. Later, we added a bushwhacker for snakes or brush.

With few constraints regarding destinations, we decided to sail to Fraser Island 125 miles north, doable in three to four days. But before departing for Fraser Island, Brisbane friends had insisted we see The Blow Hole. Here, underground saltwater more than two hundred feet from shore, compressed by underground erosion, exploded to one hundred or more feet, a variation of Old Faithful without the sulfur. The force of the salt spray put tears in my eyes and droplets on my skin. Invisible erosion, in the shape of a crescent running deep below the water table, forcibly compressed the seawater. This water moved deeply and powerfully through coral and sand, and then with increasing speed, roared upward, sometimes to one hundred and fifty feet and exploded with the force of a small bomb. It was worth the side trip.

Having experienced another natural wonder, we departed for Fraser Island, our next anchorage to be determined. A world heritage site, Fraser Island is the world's largest sand island with a seventy-five-mile beach. We anchored offshore, took the dinghy in, and anachronistically found a taxi service that helped us access some of the inland wilderness. The place remarkably demonstrated the adaptability of flora and fauna. I asked myself *How can an island of sand support rain forest trees, palms, and fern?* I later learned much of the vegetation relied on above-ground roots absorbing windblown nutrients. Decaying insects also fed the sand.

Unlimited visions of birds, butterflies, and flowers,

especially around the freshwater lakes, interrupted my vigilance for the island's dingoes. These are the purebred canines that did not crossbreed with dogs or other species on the island or mainland. Always dangerous, they attack and sometimes kill small or frail humans. On that outing, we saw only one crocodile "sleeping" along a tributary. We quietly walked the other way. Many more crocs were to follow in more isolated places.

As it turned out, Wayne decided to take advantage of a college friend's offer to stay in his Gladstone house and borrow his car. John welcomed us, opened the guest room, gave us a tour of the water filtration plant he managed, and then the keys to his car, saying, "Don't worry about washing it on its return."

We had an uneventful tour, if such an event can occur in this area. We got stuck in mud, got out of the mud, and returned to our host's home. The car was such a mess that we decided to lightly hose it down. This we did first, and then, after washing all the used dishes, sweeping the kitchen and living areas, we prepared to return to *Nyalan* the next morning. About to say goodbye, we were shocked to find John fuming, angrily saying what slobs we were.

"How can you not have cleaned the mud from the undercarriage of the car?"

Wayne defensively stuttered, "But you said, 'Don't bother washing the car.'"

He denied our defense. "Just go."

We offered to wash the undercarriage, but he again yelled, "Just go." Realizing nothing more could be done, Wayne shrugged and moved on.

We never met up with that "friend" again.

One of the more self-evident reasons that Wayne and I decided upon sailing as a lifestyle was the normally endless days free of stress with soft winds carrying us slowly and usually without drama along the eastern coast. Occasionally a 40-inch bass or a greater than arm's-length tuna hooked onto the drop lines I had hung over the stern. To me, these were truly trophy fish compared to Ohio walleyes and small mouth bass. The strength required to get the tuna to the stern demonstrated that Wayne could be a brute of a man. As he worked, he did ask for the gauntlet gloves I had brought on board anticipating, if we were successful, any deep-water fish fighting for its life. Once on board, the tuna did not give up thrashing and jumping in the now crowded cockpit. We could hardly move or navigate as we carefully avoided the powerful flopping of the fins. *What could we do?* It was then that I remembered the weapon I had brought on board. Being an Aussie, Wayne would not allow any kind of gun, so I negotiated a Louisville Slugger baseball bat that I kept hidden with my clothes. My plan was that, if any pirate boarded us, I would grab the bat and give it to Wayne to clobber the bad guy.

An alternate use ensued after I ran below and handed the bat to Wayne. The death of the tuna was a visual lesson on the fragility of life's beauty and the absolute grayness of death. This tuna, initially powerful and iridescent radiating a rainbow of color, succumbed to the blows. During that eternal minute, we were exhausted, close to tears. We watched death take over the scene.

Of course, our next task was removal and packaging of the flesh which became our primary protein source for the next week. We did not have ice nor refrigeration, but we packed it close to the hull of the boat below water level, and it remained edible.

Once again sailing north toward one of many of the small town ports, there was occasional frustration if a recommended anchorage did not provide a solid holding ground. This meant somewhere in the middle of the night, our boat arrived where we were not welcome—someone's beach house, waterfront, or in open waters without someone on watch. Probably the most inconvenient landing was the one at Airlie Beach. This rivulet, which we walked through to get to the mainland was lined with extremely sticky black mud. Our focus, balance, and lower body muscle strength countered the effect of the mud (think black glue) that stuck and weighted our shoes, our skin, our clothes, and refused to rinse off us or our dinghy. Obviously, a minor inconvenience, but nonetheless annoying.

The Whitsunday Islands proved to be my all-time favorite sailing ground. Around one hundred islands, bordered by sand so white and clean that it felt like powdered sugar marked the border of uninhabited tropical forests. I could row our dinghy to any shoreline, choosing from miles and miles of beauty undisturbed by humans. This reality without books, radio, or script, forced me to simply enjoy whatever materialized. If I took the dinghy or swam to an island wearing my bikini, I always brought fresh water and a sheer cotton sarong, so thin and small it could fit in my fist. This helped me get saltwater out of my eyes and also served as a beach blanket.

Sea birds and butterflies and lorikeets gave each landing a magical allure. The softly rolling sea provided a melodic backdrop. I sigh for that pure existence drifting mentally with soft breezes and just being. This lingers with me today. These seventy-four island parks harbor the glorious endangered reefs that are part of The Great Barrier Reef. Access to minor reefs could be done randomly from *Nyalan*, but commercial tours, most of them departing from Cairns, controlled most of the tourists as they snorkeled the reef or viewed it through glass-bottomed boats, thus minimizing human damage to the reefs These tours did not interest us because we wanted the isolation, and we never, ever touched these endangered and extremely fragile reefs with hands, feet, or flippers.

We noted the clear water magnified the sea life that

appeared as if moving spotlights were highlighting the extraordinary range of pure color and codependent life. Just as with the tuna, the dying or dead coral uncomfortably contrasted with the visible shimmer of the living sea displaying an original canvas of life in color, movement, and pattern. Later I learned some healthy corals do look pale as if dying.

The backdrop of vegetation, sea grass, sea lettuce, red and green algae, anemones, and coral varieties rhythmically set the stage. Music could be imagined. Texture, shape, color established the story to be told by the turtles, rays, clown fish, butterfly fish, starfish, eels, groupers, cod, and sea urchins. All these life forms swayed to that melody I could not hear. Mystically, in holy awe, I intensely embraced all that I could, knowing *I will never pass this way again.*

These uneventful sails, each day similar and at the same time totally different from the previous day, reset our inner clocks and tempo. Although I had brought books, paints, and music, none held my interest. Sunrise, sunset, food, and the engagement of being in "the now," being in "the moment" allowed our days to embrace the abundance of life.

Northern Australia sailing was new to Wayne. Neither of us had intensively explored any of the inland wilderness or national parks. So, we modified the plan, established safe anchorage for our primary home, *Nyalan*, and returned to Manly to pick up his sturdy Holden. This car then enabled us to meander throughout the Daintree National Park, sixty-two miles north of Cairns, and later, other remarkable territory without having to spend our savings on rental cars or having to join organized tours with their accompanying chatter of tourists.

Some campgrounds throughout Cape Tribulation, which encompassed the Daintree Parks and Mossman

Gorge, were free. The Australians had proactively design-nated five hundred national parks that covered 4 percent of their land, and then over the decades, they continued to set aside an additional 6 percent of the continent. They were devoted to protecting other undeveloped lands seeking funds from corporations, individuals, or local government for funding.

We chose to give a miss to the barge managed by a cable system that transported vehicles across the Daintree River to the western side of the park. Instead, we headed for Mossman Gorge, with its abundance of clear waterfalls and adjoining land supporting many variations in plants and animals. There were so many I could only learn about a few. Trees were relatively easy to recognize, although to differentiate between the variations of mahoganies and oaks was beyond my capability. I could remember only a few palm varieties. I loved the paperbark trees with their continuously shedding cinnamon and copper colored bark. After that day laboriously hiking the gorge, and after other self-immersions in other primitive places, I recognized a pattern in which, on reflection, I repeatedly lost my sense of self. *I am not one. I am all. Humbled by all that was and is, I often weep.*

In thinking again about the nearly oppressive growth of moisture-loving plants, I am now aware of their eternal competition to survive, to access sufficient water and light and nutrients no matter that other competitors for these same resources may be brutally wiped out. The epiphytes are not parasitic plants, but they live on the structures of the host plants, providing them access to light and light rain-fall.

The parasitic plants successfully dominate the other plants sometimes struggling with each other for survival. The Strangler Fig Trees often start as cooperative epiphytes engendering food for the host trees. But then they convert to parasites, eventually kill their hosts by sending out roots from the height of the tree. The roots appear to be flexible ropes that wrap around the host and initially travel downward, set up their own root system upon reaching the ground, and then move upward, to wrap more and more tightly around each other, eventually squeezing all nutrients, moisture, and additional height from the host. After the host dies, the successful new tree continues the cycle. I cringe when I think of this variation of that recurrent truth, survivors stand on the shoulders of those who came before us, whether a strangler fig or a human.

ANITA VLISMAS

Chapter Eleven

Another epiphyte, air plants that do not root in the soil, were the earth-grounded bromeliads. They float in small pools of water, providing shelter for tadpoles and their eggs, which then leave nutrients for other plants. The bromeliads attracted me because of their dark red centers, spear-shaped smaller leaves that enlarge beyond the tight knit center to larger more purplish, lighter colored, thorn-covered leaves. It's a great system. They provide breeding homes for smaller creatures, the size controlled by the degree of compression within the construction of the flower. These animals provide nutrients for the rootless bromeliad.

In Mossman Gorge, I finally put together my untutored knowledge about the basket ferns that I had recurrently hung inside and out of my many homes in the states. This plant I could keep alive, but it was not until my Mossman Gorge visit that I learned it wasn't my great fern-raising skill as much as their great survivability mechanisms. As parasites, they simply needed a reliable source of moisture, and they could establish their own ecosystems on the ground or in the highest branches of most rainforest trees. Again, they provided the shelter and breeding grounds, and the rats, frogs, and amphibians provided the nutrients.

Mossman Gorge was not a walk in the park. There, we climbed what, to me, were huge granite boulders varying in size from large packing crates to irregularly stacked cabins. Irregular shapes, wet surfaces, sometimes moss covered, intimidated me, so I cautiously slowed my ascent. This was not a place for my walking stick, but two-handed climbs up, over, and down. If I were a goat, it might have been more fun, but climbing upward absolutely required my state of the art, and solidly secure hiking shoes, alertness to sudden surface changes or fissures in the rocks, and sureness in my foot placements.

As I mentioned earlier, Mossman Gorge is part of Cape Tribulation. Captain Cook, the intrepid explorer, initially named the cape after Endeavour and struck coral in The Great Barrier reef. Forced to limp to Cooktown for repairs, he did not explore the cape or the gorge. Because of the terrain and inhospitable forests, he scorned the north-eastern boundary of Australia and showed little interest in this 180 million-year-old wilderness. After my own explorations, I feel connected to some of Captain Cook's tribulations, but I also appreciate his putting this peninsula on the map. He did not know Cape Tribulation was the world's oldest continuously surviving rainforest, yet he led the way in its eventual annexation to a thriving country that has conscientiously maintained this rainforest's unique position in the study of wilderness.

Wayne and I again drove north, following the Coastal Range that dropped to the sea where hundreds of miles of hopefully eternal white sandy beaches marked the eastern boundary. The one hundred miles between Cairns and Cape Tribulation can easily be driven in three hours. However, the four days we meandered between those destinations allowed daily swims in serene turquoise waters. We hiked paths established by the park rangers and by evening, we hungrily devoured meals cooked on well-built campfires, a skill we had quickly learned. The dry season deleted concerns about stormy disruptions to the rain forest's general unpredictability. As the hawks road the thermals over the sea and the koalas chewed calmly in their eucalyptus trees, unexpected kangaroos abruptly interrupted our thoughtful moments. Later we discovered that, in an instant, lorikeets and parrots could also suddenly overwhelm us flooding our awareness with rainbows of color and the screech of birds.

One extraordinary surprise did occur on a moonless night, while sleeping in our home away from home. I had to pee. Not thinking to bring a flashlight, I used my fingers to guide my movements as I touched the tent to reach its outside far corner. I then took three more unsure steps to create some distance and not disturb Wayne. My calculations placed me within the boundaries of our solitary campsite. First squatting with pants around my ankles, I peed and then started to stand when I heard a rhythmic thumping, feeling as if the earth moved. Whoosh. My heart raced. I quickly stood and pulled up my pants. Some creature had brushed my cheek. I asked myself *Is it dangerous? What could it be? Animal? Insect? Bird?*

Carefully returning to the tent, my heart was still thumping as I considered my choices. Because the creature was as high as my cheek, fast moving, heavy enough to shake the earth, and left a slight animal scent in my memory, I concluded it was a relatively small kangaroo, probably around five feet tall. No harm at all unless it knocked me down. *Oh well. Another night in the wild. Soon there will be a waxing moon.*

Advised that the most northern tip of Australia, the Cape York Peninsula, was best accessed by sea or four-wheel drive, we decided to book a two-week journey, first joining fifteen other tourists on a northbound cargo ship, and then joining two other passengers and a driver in a four-wheel drive southbound in a non- air-conditioned van. This was definitely an excellent use of our scarce dollars because this remains one of the last untouched wild places, larger than England and marked by unsealed, sand-layered, single-lane roadways sometimes crossing rivers replete with unexpected gullies and axle-breaking logs. Of course, there were always the crocodiles.

The food on the cargo ship was nothing to cause a weight gain, nor were the other passengers of interest. Most of their time was spent drinking alcohol. Touring on cargo ships is a cheap, albeit inconvenient way, to visit chains of islands, tolerable and the price is right. Ships unloaded and loaded supplies, supplying isolated ports with necessary goods and allowing for a wider distribution of their products. Our ship unloaded us on the wharves of Port Moresby, Papua New Guinea, giving us only one day to get a feeling for this country 300 miles north of Australia. Years later, I belatedly learned about the detrimental colonizing of England on those northern islands and Australia. Remarkably significant anthropological digs, discovery of unknown tribes still warring over territory in the mountains, head hunting and cannibalism were occurring a relatively short distance from the small town we walked. We were invited into the home of a British-born settler who grew Jamaican Blue Mountain coffee and collected archaeological treasures. I had learned of Blue Mountain coffee in Missouri, never dreaming I would encounter the beans in Papua New Guinea.

Present day enterprise co-existed with tribal isolation. Scientists continue research in how and why cultures and individuals survive. At departure, I might have purchased a souvenir, "a handmade genuine ceremonial face mask," but I believed it to be a derivative of latter day commercialism and gave it a miss.

My day in Port Moresby was an extension of my

seeing the New Guinea and Solomon Islanders dancing at the World Exposition in 1987. Until then, I had not realized the importance of the cape as a landing point for the Japanese invasion. The enemy managed to threaten the mainland with several submarines lurking in Sydney Harbor.

On our return, the cargo ship stopped for three more hours at Thursday Island, known as the administrative center for the Torres Strait Islands, which were initially settled by Melanesians and Polynesians. Guides at the pearl divers distribution center instructed us in the grading of pearls and the lives of free divers, many of them grandmothers. Pearl farms today allow harvesting of commercially created pearls in shallow waters without the imminent danger of sharks. The deep-diving grandmothers must have been very hungry or simply courageous.

Arriving at what was reportedly the most northern beach, we relaxed as staff unloaded our gear and had set up our tents, an enjoyable service indulging my appreciation of being pampered. Quickly, before sunset and avoiding the heat of the day, a California attorney and I walked out well beyond the tideline. We lowered ourselves to sit in two inches of water one hundred feet from shore, when we were startled by the leader of our tour group running toward us yelling and signaling with his arms to get back to shore. We did not understand. This beach appeared idyllic. Nothing was amiss. When the guide finally got to us, we finally understood he believed us to be in imminent danger. Crocodiles can quickly attack and devour unsuspecting, unguarded women chatting as the evening sun sets. We quickly returned to the campsite.

Wayne and I and our new friend Jane, the attorney, were sharing our non-air-conditioned four-wheel drive rental with a seventy-year-old man, whose silken white hair turned incongruously red within three hours on the road. Our open windows seemed to suck in unremitting billows of the reddish sand and dust covering the one-lane trail designated as a national highway.

Jane had arrived at the jeep with an oversize suitcase. Obviously awkward to load onto the top of the jeep, the suitcase became an embarrassing reminder of what this excursion was really about—pristine wilderness, unpredictable wildlife, minor physical challenges, and definitely not a costume party.

Given the circumstances, Jane announced the next morning "I am not going to change clothes this entire week. I'm wearing a sleeveless, floor-length black cotton dress. It will minimize my exposure to the dust, and I can wear it inside out if I can no longer tolerate a reddish-black dress."

She was great fun and had already invited us to recuperate at the end of the trip in her pre-rented suite at the best hotel in Cairns. We were all looking forward to a champagne celebration, but meanwhile we knew we still had much to experience.

We quickly learned to roll, bend, and keep our balance as the jeep rarely stopped jouncing for the entire week. We definitely appreciated our experienced driver as he successfully traversed rivers impeded with boulders. Sometimes we got stuck, but he had jacks and chains ready to solve the unexpected. He maneuvered inclines, slid on steep, unexpected downhill slopes, and skillfully coped with highway margins alarmingly close to cliffs butting out over the sea.

New washouts could unexpectedly vanish forty feet of National Highway One. When the road flattened, as it sometimes did between the ups and the downs and the twists and the turns, there was time to appreciate the incongruity of Japanese motorcyclists decked out in fully leather protective gear. Most of the time, the cyclists rode alone. I imagined this was a rite of passage because there were no hospitals, few vehicles, temperatures high enough to cause heart attacks, and there was only one destination, the northern tip of Australia.

Even though I had previously seen strip mining in West Virginia and later the largest in Minnesota, I was totally unprepared for the bauxite mines at Weipa, on the western side of the land mass. Digging machines, loaders, trucks, and dwarfed humans aggressively mined the rolling land, so it too was reflecting sand, now more golden in hue. Australia produces 30 percent of the world's bauxite, an essential ingredient in making aluminum. The idea of mining 3,000 million tons a year is hard to imagine. For me, the five mines in Weipa left me imagining the scarring effects on the landscape of the multitude of other mines in the world.

Returning us to the east coast, our driver gave us a historical review of the significance of Cape York and even southeastern Australia during World War II. My father-in-law had many stories of our soldiers enjoying a bit of civilization in his family restaurant and Japanese submarines lurking on the east coast, but over the evening campfire, our driver/guide now instructed us on the significance of Cape York as a barrier to the Japanese invasion and the importance of the Australian telegraph system. Prior to the war, telegraph stations dotted the land from Canberra in the extreme south, to the tip of Cape York. In the mid-1800s, the strength of the Australian dream to develop a democratic culture open to the entire world of commerce, in spite of the distances, energized men and women of all backgrounds, including the renown convicts, to raise telegraph poles and then connect them with galvanized steel wire. Whether coping with heat above one hundred degrees or the monsoons that held captive entire communities for weeks, they worked. By the late 1850s, every capital was linked, and within fifteen years, the world. In a landscape rendering little visibility of human intrusion, our passing the remains of the overland stations and poles engaged more questions for our guide. Well prepared to explain this chapter of bringing Australia into world trade, the guide was pleased to share the importance of the remaining derelict structures in the development of a new culture. The galvanized steel cables reflect a living museum after one hundred years.

Departing Cairns after the very successful commercial tour by sea and land, which had allowed access to areas we could not have negotiated on our own, Wayne and I relocated to the Holden. We drove west to the three-thousand-foot Atherton Tableland. The plateau, which was created one million years ago by volcanic eruptions, strongly contrasts to the harsh outback. It consists of some of the richest soil in Queensland. Coffee, banana, peanut, avocado, and cattle plantations all require various ecosystems, and they could flourish there because of the rich variety of soil. Calmly enjoying an easy drive in the cool, moist air, we were aiming for a gypsy colony or minimally one of the artist settlements we had heard about when suddenly Wayne accelerated, changed our course, and abruptly headed downhill.

Experiencing anaphylactic shock, Wayne was choking and wheezing. He could not talk. He would not stop. Finally, when we neared sea level, he was better and explained that he was life-threateningly allergic to wild grasses, which extensively patterned the cooler, fertile, non-cultivated areas. As a child, before asthmatic remedies were available, he had missed a year of junior high school, too weak to leave his bed. This current experience reminded him of his other overall allergic vulnerabilities, which had not appeared because he rarely visited grasslands.

High drama, sometimes life threatening, followed by moments of calmness and bliss, seemed to be our pattern. The next time we set up camp, having relocated south and west, the evening was uneventful, but then, the next morning's sun, created more drama.

The lush tree we had chosen for protection from heat was dropping deadly green ants and missing Wayne, so far. He rapidly retreated to the protection of the car as I hastily packed. Later, over breakfast, he prepared me for a later experience with even more dangerous red fire ants. In that future time, after only one bite, even with a heavy dose of Benadryl, Wayne passed out on our sleeping bags, and I counted ninety-two quarter-sized swellings from his head to his feet. Little wonder that the sea was his chosen environment. I wondered why he would expose himself to such attacks, but then, was this any riskier than my acceptance of possible snake bites, crocodile attacks, or drownings at sea?

Leaving the rainforests and palm trees, we continued south, departing Highway One for the backroads, winding by cattle stations populated by 2,000-pound bulls and hundreds of cows. We never saw the ranch houses. In this savannah, which was not a danger to Wayne, termite mounds taller than our vehicle appeared so often we began to take them for granted. Deriving nutrients from guano, (bird droppings) and moisture from deep under the ground, the termites sometimes dug so deeply that water was released and percolated upward, thus nurturing the survival of many life forms, despite the extreme heat.

What awes me as I review my focus on termites surviving in temperatures deadly to most animals is that this new interest reminds me of my passion as a young girl when I collected and studied city spiders. I was fascinated by their hiding places and the extraordinarily strong yet extremely fine and detailed webs spun by the spiders that are usually considered vile.

What is this all about? I asked myself then and in that lowland. How could spiders survive in the concrete of cities created by humans? How and why do the termites survive in wastelands throughout the planet? They initially appear useless, yet they build incredibly elaborate, solid mounds resembling the architecture of European cathedrals, and easily reach twenty-five vertical feet. Many termite species, and there are more than three thousand, design their colonies facing magnetic north and south, a behavior anyone has yet to explain. Like spiders, they endure the most hostile environments on earth. Like all creatures, even when individual colonies die there remain reminders of the birth and death of those individual colonies.

This can be seen in the debris layered with the carcases of the dead. A scientist might also determine the birth of new colonies by observing slightly different DNA. A slight difference in DNA might enhance survival probabilities of a new species. For three million years, termites, like cockroaches, have and will survive. They present as solitary independent creatures, but like all of us, they are integral, and they nurture the survival of multitudes of other creatures throughout our planet. In addition to tapping and storing moisture deep in the extensive below-ground structures, they absorb what they need and recycle the remaining, reprocessed nutrients to countless desert creatures such as birds, frogs, ants, and mice. Guano bird droppings are always an extremely rich source of minerals as the cycle goes on.

Having pitched camp in another innocuous, clean, almost grassy campground, Wayne and I slept well and awakened to white clouds, birds, and warm, not torrid, sun. We rolled the bedrolls anticipating breaking camp when I was horrified, staring at a twelve-inch hole in the floor of the tent. *Some thing was trying to get us. But what?* No visible critter, scat, or feathers indicated what it could have been, but pragmatically aware, we were unharmed, seemingly without body damage or disease. Only "disappeared" tent fabric and a tiny section of the blanket indicated we had a visitor or visitors.

So, what's the thing do? Onward with our adventure, and maybe the mystery will come to light. Upon meeting locals, we always brought up our dilemma. We explained we had mended the hole with duct tape, but we still wanted to know what had penetrated our ostensibly safe boundaries. What could we do to prevent another attack from the unknown? We did not fuss much about it; however, we always fastened the zipper securely.

Weeks later, we were still on the quest to identify our intruder(s) when an Aussie casually announced, "Oh, you were infiltrated by corbie grubs. They are a gardener's nuisance, destroying lawn because they breed like caterpillars. They liked you two because you were warm, and it was their time to lay eggs."

Now that we knew our intruders were not dangerous, we coped by simply placing a second tarp under the tent until we were setting up the tent on more grub-hostile ground cover—rocks, hard-packed dirt, and sand.

As we continued on the main highway south along the eastern seaboard, smoke filled our non-air conditioned car. We kept the windows open. Hypnotic, twenty-foot flames roared above three-inch-wide sugar cane stalks that continued to support the elongated sooty green leaves standing four- to ten-feet tall. I took time to name the hues I could see: Orange, violet, peach, purple, blue, yellow, a fiery rainbow.

The growers' intention before the harvest was to kill weeds and vermin, including poisonous snakes, invasive shiny green frogs, and the gnarly brown cane toads. These nuisances were intrusive to human settlements and known for surprising appearances in suburban swimming pools. They also were nuisances to the aboriginals. Their community houses provided showers and the luxury of flush toilets, an outside source of income. Upon looking forward to sitting on a comfortable, modern commode, I opened a stall door to a bowl heaped to the edge with brilliant, beautiful, out-of-place green frogs. Every one of the eight stalls offered more frogs in each bowl. I asked myself *how would it ever be possible to flush?*

Sometimes traveling away from the main highway, side roads led us to other examples of aboriginal enterprise. Their art, always beautiful in its representations of aboriginal tales of the Rainbow Serpent is believed as history. Museums were a treat for us, and we were pleased to pay to enter. For the locals, art was not the only source of income. They adapted to white man's ways. If a problem does not exist, create one, so a solution can be sold to those with dollars. In aboriginal country, the rivers could normally be forged by auto slowly and with care. Enterprising aboriginals constructed dams from rocks and brush, widened, and excavated deeper parts of the creeks, and filled them with unseen boulders or dead tree trunks. Upon arriving at these traps, we smiled at the idyllic children laughing and playing as their elders sat in dilapidated lawn chairs placed in six-inches of water, keeping their feet cool. They peacefully waited for prey. We, the unsuspecting, fell for the trap twice, the second time when the entrepreneurs hid in the bushes, not warning us. Of course, for a fee, there was always sufficient assistance to get us out of the hole and across the river.

In a more populated small town, an art gallery rustically built with unfinished timber and twelve-foot-high walls lured me. I was expecting more aboriginal creations, the stuff for tourists. This was different. Ten- by eight-foot canvases were representing a one-woman show. The artist, a twenty-seven-year-old art school graduate, worked with acrylics, broad brushes, and these huge canvases. The content and design were masterful in use of color, design, movement, and especially meaningful content.

Her recurrent theme was seen in the images of Mac

Tractor Trailer Trucks speeding down highways, destroying butterflies, an artist's vision of reality and metaphor. Ironically, Wayne's uncles owned a fleet of Mac trucks, the name coming from his maternal side of the family. When we purposely returned to the museum, her work was down, and someone told me she had moved to another town. I could not find her and wanted more. Her commentary on Australia's environmental changes still echoes when I see a butterfly or tractor trailers speeding down the Long Island Expressway. Few butterflies experience the sun along this highway.

Next, meandering toward Sydney, where siblings, aunts and uncles resided, we were happy to plan a family picnic to finally celebrate our marriage with Wayne's family. We spread the food and ourselves on two red, yellow, and green wool plaid blankets in a shady park overlooking the city. We drank the champagne Wayne and I provided. I was disappointed there were no gifts, not even small tokens of recognition of our marriage. It was not an issue of money. Two of his siblings and partners were economists, two were architects, one a chemist, one a landscape architect, and his parents still had a business. I attributed this benign neglect to cultural differences, but in my heart, I really knew better because Wayne's sisters had had big wedding parties. Perhaps it was their jealousy of our nonconformity. I never discussed the slight with Wayne. We went on with our wonderful lives and did not bother with feelings of neglect.

Chapter Twelve

As we continued on the main highway south and then west, our explorations into the wilds of Australia provided other opportunities to observe wild animals in their natural habitat. I had known about most of them, even the rat kangaroo, a marsupial, that is the smallest kangaroo and looks like a huge New York City rat. We could occasionally see it grazing, backlit by the setting sun. Recurrently dingoes, which were feral dogs impossible to domesticate, came into the news by running off with an aboriginal's child or occasionally intruding into a small-town neighborhood. But the dingoes had not bothered us, and because of their reputation for aggressive ferocity, we did not bother them. However, after absorbing the iridescent colors of native butterflies, particularly the sapphire and black Ulysses wonder, much of my interest in sighting the more common creatures was sated.

Hoping to see the purportedly extinct Tasmanian Tiger, at least in a museum, was a minor reason we took the ferry with our reliable Holden and camping gear to Tasmania. I had been disappointed to learn about the Tasmanian Tiger's extreme vulnerability in the modern world. I had seen surviving marsupials, kangaroos, possums, and wombats, and finally realized I would never see a living Tasmanian Tiger. I had read that both sexes carry their young in their pouches, and they look like elongated dogs with rising hips and distinctive stripes. Around the time I was born, the naturalists published definitive articles stating that the last of this species, cared for in the Tasmanian Zoo, was extinct. After our trip, we learned there had been new sightings on the mainland.

Having ferried to Hobart and eaten the famous blue oysters, we arrived at a commercial campground. The manager gave us directions to a hiking trail—medium difficulty. We anticipated walking four to six hours, counted on trail markers, and left midday. Medium difficulty proved to be an absolute misnomer. We encountered an alpine glacier where we expected a narrow, rocky trail. The snow was wet, shallow, and slippery. Wayne, always confronting his height phobias, crumbled. The distance, perhaps only an eighth of a mile wide, with eight inches of snow, needed to be traversed on a thirty-degree incline. It was too late to return the way we had come.

He, red in the face, voice trembling, called "What do I do?"

At that moment, I passed him, traversing on all fours, fingers and toes dug into the snow. I laughingly yelled, "Honey, just watch my bum and place your hands and feet where I will mark a safe path. Just follow my trail and watch me wiggle."

He did. I did. We thought the rest of the hike would be easy.

However, in Tasmania, trails described as medium difficulty create surprises for those with moments of hubris. I probably deserved my souvenir incurred in the next ten minutes. The descending path, steep and even more rocky, required strength exceeding my own. I slipped, scraped but did not break my left patella. The now-bloody trail offered Wayne something else to worry about. We continued even more cautiously because the sun was dropping quickly. We entered our camp relieved and administered first aid to my knee. Thirty years later, the one by two inch horizontal scar remains a tangible souvenir.

We moved our camp to higher ground, Cradle Mountain. Lorikeets and wild parrots again crowded us, maniacally fluttering as if in attack mode, and then perching on our heads and shoulders as if we were warm, friendly trees. Settling in, we carefully asked other hikers about the difficulty of the trail and quickly learned that, other than the need for strength and balance, which I could compensate for with my walking stick, we would need to deal with leeches. *Oh no. Not again? Ha. I'm prepared.* I had thrown two pairs of gaiters into our bags.

When hiking in wet areas or requiring protection from deep snow and ice, outdoor lovers dress for the occasions and when indicated, strap on their gaiters, water- and leech-repellent ankle, shin, knee protectors. The other hikers had incurred leeches, but with their gaiters, they were unaffected. Our gaiters also protected us. The day before our return to Melbourne, during an ordinary walk on a well-groomed trail, I saw what I believed was a small black cat about sixty feet away, rhythmically trotting forward on the trail. I was watching and following him carefully, intentionally maintaining the distance and remaining as nonintrusive as possible. Confused by the animal's bright red ears, I thought I was seeing a different species of the usual domestic feline. Not so. That day, I had experienced one of those rare sightings of the Tasmanian Devil in the wild.

I did not know this until, returning to camp, I found a picture of it in the guidebook. It was described as a "dog-like" marsupial, weighing about seven pounds. The photograph in the book was identical to the "cat" I saw, right down to the red ears. "Tasmanian Devils are not dangerous unless attacked," the guidebook said. *Wow. Did I feel special? Absolutely.* I knew only a few hikers ever saw this rarity, and I was totally pleased with myself, a classic book-worm who simply wanted to camp, sleep outside, and embrace every new experience. This was another of many yet to come.

I was a stranger in this new world of abundance, and I often found it difficult to focus on any one thing in detail. It would have been impossible for anyone, and it was even more so for a hyper visual like me. Restraint is not my usual mode of operation. Yet unlike my usual style of inquiry, I had taken the time to see something different from the expected, to follow it quietly, and note enough details so I could later make a positive identification.

I have never talked about that sighting until this book. I felt no reason to share it. If I had, it might have sounded as if I were bragging.

In the Snowy Mountains of Mt. Kosciuszko Park, the 2,000-foot range is the tallest in mainland Australia, supporting at least five ecosystems. I was excited to be there, having seen the movie *The Man From Snowy River* in the early 1980s. It was an unexceptional western with a memorable scene of the young, virile hero crashing down the jagged mountain on a beautiful black stallion. That was the hook for me to drive through those summer snow-laden ski slopes. We were alone, camped on a rocky, ragged slope abandoning our search for level ground on which we could pitch the tent. We were eating a full breakfast of fried eggs and pancakes with fresh cowboy coffee, the kind we just boiled in the billy. I was sitting on a sun-warmed rock, holding my plate and enjoying the moment. There were no tables. Just rocks and the downhill view of a few tall trees with a dense undergrowth of heath and an occasional glimpse of bogs.

At that moment, Wayne said, very quietly, "You may want to slowly get up and walk toward me. There is a brown snake next to you."

This time, I calmly followed his directions. Later, he told me the eastern brown snake is the second most venomous snake in Australia, and mine was about five-feet long. Only then did I realize that this was possibly a close call, but I thought W*hat the hell. It's a done deal, and we are all right.* We carefully broke camp and did not hike farther.

On the return, we drove through Canberra, the national capital, which is awkwardly located halfway between Melbourne and Sydney. It remains small compared to the more densely populated cities. Slow to show the aging of mature buildings, its efficiently designed neighborhoods and street grids are in place to receive future populations.

Finally back on *Nyalan*, we began speaking about future plans. We had decided we loved this lifestyle, but we wanted a larger yacht. This meant we had to go to work as we intended to stay with our plan, "Save the principal and still live well."

We asked ourselves, "Are we to remain in Australia or live two years here and then two years in US?"

We decided I should try once again to find work in Australia, given I was now married to an Australian citizen. To our surprise, I received a response to my application for a placement in Adelaide, the capital of South Australia. After a brief phone call to the Department of Human Services, the hiring official agreed to fly us from Brisbane so we might interview in person. We were excited to have this unexpected gift of a two-day expense account, an opportunity to visit the famous wine country of the Barossa Valley and a peek into the social services available in a city first developed in the mid-1800s. We even checked out housing, some of which was impressively Victorian. This was affordable.

The interview went well. They were prepared to hire me, and then I began to really think seriously about this alternative life choice. *Wayne could always find work, but I would now be 10,000 miles away from my children and their families. The work was important, creating better lives for people in need of help, but it would be more of the same for me, and the weather was killingly hot.* I awkwardly gave my answer before flying back to Queensland. My lasting memory was not one of total guilt but included our late-afternoon visit to the seventy-shop fully air conditioned city center arcade. It was so cool with glittering individualized shops displaying products from clothes, jewels, luggage, fish, cheeses, meats, breads, produce, and anything else shoppers might want. The arcade provided unexpected relief to that impossible heat with its smells of foods and sometimes sweaty people, sounds of happy shoppers and background music, impeccable tile floors, and highly polished display cases.

About to leave for the states, Wayne and I remembered we were not carrying health insurance, so we made appointments for complete physical check-ups. This was when we learned that Wayne, now thirty-six years old, had "funny blood." The doctor was vague. "Go on and enjoy your lives," he said. Wonderful advice. It permitted us to live without the reality of a foreboding cloud over our days.

Wayne stayed behind, wanting to sell *Nyalan* before his departure. I went ahead, planning to spend ten days in New Zealand using the bus system to see the southern island. The public bus driver planned rest stops so passengers might see some of the sights. After peacefully walking through a small extremely green forest with ground covered entirely in moss and four-foot ferns, I named this place The Ballroom Floor. It was meant for waltzing.

Continuing to Queenstown, I saw sheep grazing on

every available hillside and construction workers wearing shorts and knee-high mud boots. In Queenstown, I booked into a new backpackers' hostel, four to a room. Bunks smelled of freshly cut wood, and the rooms shined with new varnish. At breakfast, I made arrangements for three twenty-year-old hikers to keep an eye on me as I followed them in a climb up one of many isolated hiking trails. Obviously, their skills and strength far exceeded my own, so within an hour, we agreed they would continue up this lonely incline, and I would follow at my own pace. If they did not meet me on their return and I had not returned to the hostel by late afternoon, they would send out a search party. Our hikes were uneventful and that night we celebrated with beer.

Another day, I booked passage on a twenty-seat boat touring Milford Sound, where we could see waterfalls, mountains, glaciers and, unexpectedly, a tipped kayak with two passengers swimming for their lives in freezing water. Our tour boat turned to save them as all our passengers scrambled from their seats to get a better view of the action. Passengers and crew were not aware that the change in weight distribution was tipping our boat. We were already inclined twenty degrees.

I stood up and yelled, "Return to your seats. You are going to sink our boat." At the top of my school teacher's voice, I again ineffectively yelled, "Return to your seats." The crew finally caught on and with a loudspeaker directed our passengers to their seats.

The crew dropped a ladder, two nearly drowned, and very wet kayakers were soon seated in our main cabin, their bodies covered with blankets. Obviously thankful they had lived and we just happened to be in the area where they had tipped, they were admonished by the captain that this was definitely the wrong time of the year for kayaking.

Soon after, I bused from Queenstown to Christchurch

and then to Auckland. I flew to Florida and opening my mail in my parents' house, I was surprised and pleased I had received a job offer to join an HMO (health management organization) as a clinical psychologist. Cigna paid for me to fly to San Francisco and house me during the required one-week's training and orientation. I knew the room would be big enough for two, so Wayne and I paid for his airline ticket and enjoyed a San Francisco vacation. Because we used the daily stipend to buy meals at the deli, we even had enough money to buy two bottles of medium-priced wine. We also had time in the evening to see San Francisco, not missing the bridge haloed with dramatic night lights. We chuckled at our cleverness. What fun we had for the price of Wayne's flight.

There were fifty new hires in the room where training occurred. I was particularly attracted to Allison. We were the trouble makers. Quietly, we questioned the procedures being imposed on their model of therapy. We could see that a lot of the rules of the organization were not for the benefit of the clients, but we went along with it, only occasionally challenging the speakers in public. We wanted the work. We were allies in our discontent with the controls being established over experienced psychologists. We grumbled quietly between ourselves. She was assigned to Miami and I to Florida's west coast. I believe the strength of our bonding was not only based on our working experience, but more important, we were both blue-water sailors. *What a coincidence.*

Wayne and I visited Allison and a friend in her uncle's mansion located next to a Donald Trump villa. Later, when they had sailed through the keys on their way across the Gulf, they visited us. Unfortunately, on their sail to Mexico, they encountered high seas, the boat floundered for ten days, she was sick, weak, and pregnant. She almost died. A movie was eventually made about this high drama.

I never saw it.

Now established in Florida, I continued to work for Cigna, sometimes being on call for forty-eight hours along with normal clinic hours. Sometimes a night call would come from an out-of-county hospital, and I was required to drive perhaps thirty-five miles at three in the morning. In the emergency room, I often determined whether the new admissions were primarily alcoholic, depressed, demented, or simply violent. My evaluation would determine whether the individual would be treated, and which part of the insurance policy would be charged. During two months of being on call and then seeing clients during the day, I lost thirty-five pounds. I was happy to move on to different work as an independent contractor consulting in assisted living and nursing home programs, sometimes training nurses or policemen, or testing in public schools. To draw on various sources of income, I retained my license in school psychology. I also rented a small office to see private clients. Thank goodness Wayne was available to garner and manage the accounts receivable as he maintained his own full-time job.

By 1994, we sold our redecorated house with all the bougainvillea and night-blooming jasmine we had planted. We had already harvested the fig, lemon, lime, orange, and grapefruit trees. We were ready to buy our new home, a seaworthy blue-water yacht. We had yet to determine which make and model.

Again, keeping costs at a minimum, we drove north to say goodbye to the Ohio and New York families. We had asked my son if we could store a few belongings in his unused coal cellar. This included Wayne's Wedgewood, and heavy stainless steel pots and pans, and afghans knitted by my grandmother and her embroidered tablecloths. Of course, I had to leave my typewriter there as well. Not much, but enough to start again should we return to land.

In addition to long-term investments, we had $100,000 cash. We loaded the Subaru with our worn camping equipment and headed toward Washington DC, which we figured was close to boat brokers on the eastern shore. This would be winter camping. We knew there was a free national park on the northern side of the city where we could pitch the tent. Light snow was falling as we made a quick cold cereal breakfast, skipped the coffee and got into the car. We drove to Annapolis. There was a marina. There was a broker's sign. We entered.

"What are you looking for?" the smart-assed salesman asked Wayne. "Power or sail? How big? How much do you have to spend? How do you want to use it? Something with bells and whistles?"

Wayne, slow to respond, gave me time to redirect and I said, "What are you talking about? Bells and whistles?" He finally noticed me.

At our own pace, we told him our goal and asked him to look around, anywhere in the states.

He asked for our phone number.

"We do not have a phone," Wayne told him.

Annoyed, he asked, "How can you buy a boat without a phone?"

"We have the dollars." I said.

Then he asked, "Well, what is your address?"

I said, "We're living in a tent in the national campground near DC."

"You can't buy a boat if you're living in a tent."

"Watch us," I said. "If you don't want the business, we'll go elsewhere"

Wayne, calm as usual, nudged me and quietly said, "Let me handle this. We're here, and maybe he can use his connections to find us something suitable." To the dealer, he said, "We will call you tomorrow and see what you turn up." This we did. The salesman had located an $80,000, 39-

foot, canoe stern, 1983 Southern Cross, one of the eighteen hulls ever built. It was designed for long-distance sailing, had a six-foot draft and eleven-foot beam. Solid and definitely seaworthy, it was described as "needing work" having sailed from Chicago, down the Mississippi and now located at a marina in Houston, Texas.

When we arrived, we could immediately see "the work." The vinyl headliner, filled with water, was sagging. Porthole gaskets leaked water, stainless rod rigging shed rust, and frayed ropes needed replacement. Besides replacing the rotten plywood of the ceiling and covering it with new vinyl, I anticipated another job I could manage. I would buy a plane to even the gullied teak, six-inch coaming. After an offshore tryout of the 29 HP Yanmar diesel engine and a review of the general mechanics and electronics, we kind of knew what we were buying as we sent the dealer the money. We put the boat *on the hard*, also called a wooden cradle, and bought a tall, folding ladder which I promptly labeled with our new, wonderful home's name, *Anita*. We chose the name *Anita* for three reasons. Because I was a US citizen, we registered *Anita* in my name to avoid state taxes. I also believed no one else would ever name a boat after me and I liked the idea, and finally, *Anita* had only five letters. Professionally painted boat names were paid for by the number of letters. As we were always cost conscious, we chose a short name.

Houston was almost as hot as some of our Australian locations. Early on Wayne put in a large air conditioner under the navigation table and we began taking siestas during the midday heat. This worked. We worked and within a few months we were ready to depart via the Texas Intracoastal Waterway to the Gulf of Mexico. We sailed past acres of wind turbines and off shore oil wells. Fortunately we were approaching Lake Pontchartrain, New Orleans when we had engine trouble. This was great as we had time to visit New Orleans, buy bialys, see the Garden District and be flooded with the constancy of live jazz.

Anita was again ready to follow our plan to sail New Orleans to Bradenton, Florida (north of Sarasota). We regretted leaving a memorable discovery. We had located a dock workers' smoky restaurant and discovered three dollar oyster *Po Boys*, the best in my entire life, juicy with freshness, fragrant with frying. We went to that dive five times for their oysters before our departure.

Crossing the Gulf was uneventful. My four-hour watches were tedious and I was absolutely pleased to have an unexpected guest as Wayne rested. A small bird flew on board and stayed for the week. I named him Freddy the Finch, offered water and grain, and gained a different kind of consciousness with an up close and personal diminutive creature. He chirped, balanced on the lifelines, pooped on the hatch cover and provided unexpected companionship. I can still feel my loss as he abruptly flew away as quickly as he had arrived, just before we could see the Florida coast. He must have been able to see or at least smell the land. Today small birds that light on my deck railing always bring back fond memories of Freddy the Finch.

We visited Kurt and family in Sarasota and invited his mother-in-law and friend to dinner on *Anita*. Then we headed south to the keys only to be stalled by cold, cold weather. It was almost freezing and a hull surrounded by cold water did not keep the sun's heat. We anticipated using our diesel furnace, something we had not yet tested. Of course, it was not working. So, we improvised heating guardedly with the galley stove, oven door open. The weather had warmed when we anchored off Key West, famous for Hemingway and his favorite bar Sloppy Joe's. We anchored between an island and the main town using our dinghy, with its eight HP duel stroke engine to carry us and two bicycles to the mainland. The bikes had been tied to the forward deck since Houston.

After using the bikes to carry dirty sheets, towels and clothes to and from the laundromat, we stored our replenished food inventory under the main salon's benches. With chores completed we were free to meander the side streets and stop in small market areas ordering strong Cuban coffee in remarkably tiny cups. I used lots of sugar. What a kick. What a treat sitting at the sidewalk watching all the locals watch us.

We did not pay for entrance to Hemingway's house or to Truman's winter home, but we did tour the environs. Pink, turquoise, yellow, stuccoed small houses lined littered streets. There was no grass except for the yards of incongruously gated estates. The villagers sat on their small porches or under their few trees and seemed to enjoy the idea of "Mañana, mañana."

We continued to safe anchorages throughout most of the inner and outer Caribbean Islands, too many for me to name or remember. One followed the other, another variation of mañana, mañana. These landings were duly noted in the ship's log and remain on today's navigation charts. Town folks were accommodating to live aboard sailors. However, the ten dollar uncooked chickens and two dollar fresh apples gave us no pleasure. We ate our own tinned or dried foods. In Houston I had purchased a sewing machine as there had been a lot of canvas repairs needed. Now our inventory needed further organization if we were to eventually sail to Nova Scotia and cross the Atlantic. We needed non-bulky, cloth containers to store sets of wrenches, screw drivers, saw blades, sewing equipment, or filters large and small. These I successfully made. However, anticipating future needs for fresh water, I also made a canvas rain collector which, when hung properly over the boom and hatch, was intended to collect fresh water. Unfortunately, this was not a success and eventually we had to actually buy water.

A twenty-four-year-old Ohio nephew flew in to join us in one of the islands' safe harbors. Taking the dinghy to shore we enjoyed a restaurant meal and returned with our rented car to the anchorage. Winds had increased, visibility was poor. We had forgotten to put on the masthead light so even finding *Anita* in the heavily clouded rain with winds aggressively buttressing our eight-foot dinghy made hard work for three adults. *Anita* had dragged dangerously close to the rocky shore. We heaved the oars and with the balance of younger sailors, we thankfully climbed onboard *Anita*.

Meanwhile winds insistently continued to push us toward shore. The anchor continued to drag. Wayne started the engine, intending to weigh anchor and move to a safer location. He could gain no purchase as our anchor was now entangled with another.

We even considered diving down and cutting it, but there were no lights, the night was black, and the rain was slashing our faces. Most important, the entanglement of our boat was caused by chain. Even if we did dive down, we could not release ourselves with a knife. Water levels in the cockpit were increasing. The bilge pump ceased pumping. We got out the long pump handle, and Adam, the stalwart, frightened youngster, started pumping, When he tired, I took my turn, comparatively a wimp. This went on for more than an hour. Wayne was still goosing the engine, trying to untangle our anchor from the other. We were possibly sinking or crashing onto the shore. Through the wind, I finally yelled, "We're okay. It's only a boat. It can sink. We can swim to shore. Put on your life jackets."

Adam remained sweating, pumping, terrified. He had never sailed before and had looked forward to a blissful Caribbean holiday. Fearing imminent threat to his life, this first experience was a bit over the top. We made it through the night. The next morning we could see that our water cooling system had cracked and caused the enormous leak. As long as the engine was on, more water flowed into the boat.

The next day, Sunday morning, our task was to find a replacement tube about six feet by five inches. Surprisingly, we found a shop that had material we could modify and use. During this search, we crisscrossed the island, and then, we saw the extensive damage this storm had created. A local man had died in his unconsidered attempt to cross a low-hung bridge during the height of the storm. Wind had blown his red truck into the sea. No one saw the man go in. No one saved him.

An unplanned holiday occurred in Nassau. We spent a day in Atlantis, a luxurious tourist destination, without renting a cabin. We anchored near the resort's beach and swam to shore. We enjoyed the clean waters with human mermaids swimming in filtered pools. We walked in the manmade streams and then sat under sun deflecting umbrellas, each of us clasping a pina colada. The alcohol soothed us into another way of being.

The islands were "much of a muchness" as the Aussies would say, similar in small populations and most landscapes. However, each island was also different because the surviving generations, whose enslaved ancestors were shipped to the islands to harvest coffee and sugar, retained their respective identities. They worked on the newly created plantations which, because of the free labor, exponentially increased the wealth of enterprising colonists. Fortunately, the slaves retained some of their prior identity, their language, their ceremonies and sometimes their beliefs in shamans and voodoo. As we listened to radio on the boat and on land, we could not miss the dominant influence of Christianity. Usually there was only one available radio station. Programming rarely included the news, only

Christian hymns.

The excitement of finding new, safe harbors and meeting other sailors with their own remarkable stories, entertained us. Some of our new acquaintances were land-based, and others were sailors. One sailing family had a seven-year-old daughter who, like many, was being home schooled. The girl and I drew and painted together on *Anita* sharing my inventory of little used artist supplies. All of her pictures were full of active movement as was her life — moving boats, either sailing yachts or power, wind-surfers, sea doo speedsters, airplanes, flying birds and fish, people waving, whether hello or goodbye, I never knew. The family had come to the keys from Germany on a WW II cruiser, inherited from a grandfather. Large windows, not portholes, enclosed the navigation station and the small dining table in the well-lit cabin made it a home. It was as comfortable as a small house. However, I always wondered about its off shore stability.

Another sailing couple we kept company with, were in my mind too obese to survive at sea, but this they did. They had little money. She made paintings using pastel chalk and sold them wherever she could. I remember going into a gallery with her as she offered her creations for sale. The gallery owners were extremely vigilant and wary, apparently fearful we might steal from them. They paid little for the few paintings she sold, but it was not the money or the recognition that was important. Freedom to follow their dream, to continue their adventure kept them sailing. They may have been old. They may have been fat. It did not matter.

Chapter Thirteen

Soon we presented our passports and ship's registration to Miami customs where we anchored for a while. The 2000 mile distant northern shores, Maine and Nova Scotia, captured our imagination. We hungered for the large mussels known to cling to rocks often scraping boat bottoms. We looked forward to our mornings in Maine when we merely had to reach overboard and harvest. After gifting me state of the art Helly Hansen underwear for my prior year's birthday, Wayne now outdid himself with a gift of a brand new lobster trap. It worked, and of course, we savored. We sparkled as we lived a variation of the lives of the Carnegies and Rockefellers.

News of an approaching storm left us again looking for a secure and safe anchorage. All the marked anchorages were taken. Fortunately, the East Harbor harbor master directed us to a sunken tractor which served our needs for that storm. Wayne merely had to dive down to the tractor and attach our anchor. Afterward, dense fog presented both novelty and a different challenge as we continued to Nova Scotia. It was our first opportunity to use our radar and I felt as if I were on a military expedition uninterruptedly powering north to the beep, pause, beep, pause, sound of radar. Fast flowing eighteen-foot tides shattered any delusion that this was a cake walk. However, we prevailed.

Now redirecting our destination southward and then east, we stopped at the Hinckley boat yard to shop and dream about more elaborate yachts. We also filled the diesel fuel tanks anticipating a quick departure from Long Island. After saying goodbyes to family, we headed for the Azores.

About eight hundred miles off shore, our engine choked and stopped. No amount of coaxing, filtering, throttle adjustments, or swearing changed the situation. Three Nor'easters headed toward us from slightly different directions, creating the effect of an environmental washing machine. Anticipating trouble and needing an unencumbered deck, Wayne masterfully threw the bicycles overboard.

No snow but freezing rains poured off the deck and us. Top of the line Gill foul weather gear with our Helly Hansen underwear provided minimal comfort as we took turns managing 30- to 40-foot waves that might have pitch poled us into oblivion. The two bilge pumps we had installed after the previous island storm kept pumping. The storm demanded all of our energy.

And then, in the midst of a situation already worthy of alarm, we argued. Without power, I wanted to wait the storm out and use our five sails to continue to the Azores. He did not. We managed to remain somewhat calm as we crashed and twisted with the waves in that environmental washing machine. Without a working depth finder, Wayne would have none of it. He refused to travel east and repeat Captain Cook's debacle on the Australian coral reefs. I refused to be rescued. Alternatively, I again suggested we wait the storm out and then drift south on prevailing winds to the Bahamas. Again, he refused, demonstrating the caution of an engineer, who with one wrong decision might kill hundreds.

So, we turned on the EPIRB—Emergency Position Indicating Radio Beacon—used for search and rescue. Although my pride pushed me towards rejecting the plan, I did realize Wayne's choice had to be fifty percent of the decision. This truth allowed me to accept his use of the EPIRB and impending rescue. With experience, I was becoming more cautious and had increased our inventory to now include two EPIRBS, one for back-up.

The Greek cargo carrier powered a day and a half to reach us. From their upper deck, twice as high as our mast, officers and deck hands dropped hawsers. We held fast as a rope ladder followed. One of the Philippine deck hands quickly climbed down to assist me in climbing the swinging ladder as Wayne stabilized the hawsers. With waves unpredictably crashing everywhere, I could not balance enough to even mount the bottom rung of the ladder. Everything was moving. I could not safely step off our deck. Next, the cargo ship's officers dropped a steel ladder which mounted diagonally along their hull and provided relatively safe access to the upper deck. My personal escort now followed me upward keeping his hands ready to thwart any possible loss of balance.

Assigned to the absent owner's cabin, we gratefully accepted the captain's invitation to dine with the five Greek officers, ignoring our preference for islander food. We took off our salt-soaked outer gear and dined in our long johns. I felt conspicuous, but hunger prevailed over modesty. For the next ten days I ate with the officers and stayed in our assigned cabin. The four-page, month-old, Greek newspaper did not entertain me, but I was safe. There was nothing to read. There was no radio. I was usually alone. Meanwhile, Wayne had a great time with the guys spending hours on the bridge. We tugged securely tied *Anita* toward

Norfolk Harbor, Virginia, as the cargo ship's hull relentlessly cracked our $20,000 mast. Then, one morning we awakened to see *Anita* independently sailing about one mile south along the Virginia coast line. Her attempted escape failed as she was again brought back to the cargo carrier to wait for custom's clearance.

Now legally in the United States, we knew our challenge was to remove all remnants of storm and salt water damage from *Anita*. Not discouraged, we knew muscles and patience would take care of this problem. This was merely a matter of work and money. We would buy a new mast.

It was then that I took time to drive from our temporary housing in Maryland to Long Island following the complicated birth of my fifth grandchild. I arrived at my son's home. Opening their kitchen door, I immediately saw Cole gasping. As Diane siphoned phlegm from my grandson's nose, she continued talking on the phone to the pediatrician. He advised patience. I waited and observed for ten more minutes. This was a difficult situation for me. I was a mother in law, not Diane's mother. Controlling myself no longer, whatever the repercussions, I finally said, "This child is seriously ill. He can't breathe. We must take him to the ER."

She argued, "It's premature. What do we do with the boys?"

I answered, "No. It's time to go, I will drive all of us."

"I'll have to get his bunting on."

"There's no time. Wrap him in a blanket."

Just then Aaron unexpectedly walked in, understood the situation, grabbed the child and his wife, and left the older children with me. The three of them were speeding to the local hospital when Cole stopped breathing— totally. Diane gave mouth to mouth respiration as Aaron redirected to the fire department. The ambulance drivers had the hospital staff waiting. Cole survived only to almost die again from a different life-threatening infection. He was medivacked to a more specialized hospital. The parents stayed with their infant. I took care of the others.

Weeks later Cole was sent home. Subsequently my return visits had me thinking *This child is not right. Despite what the MD's were saying, he seemed to me to be too good. He just sits there not going through the movements I had considered when I conducted infant evaluations decades earlier. There was little I could do at that time.* Wayne was already presenting his own difficulties. Wayne's weakness continued to confound us. *Why would a burley, strong-shouldered captain be unable to turn a lug nut that our rigger, (the skinny guy who climbs the mast), can do easily?*

The local MD in Maryland could not tell us why he was weak. This was not good enough. I asked "Who do you most respect as a cancer doc? Who's been your best teacher in the treatment of cancer?" The words "funny blood" had lingered in my memory following our last visit to an Australian MD.

Washington Hospital Center's department head and a renowned MD elaborated that Wayne's "funny blood" would probably lead us in one of three possible directions, none of them good. Leukemia loomed. He advised us "Live fully. Enjoy the day." We were good at that.

To access US health insurance, Wayne was pleased to accept a high-paying position with the DC Metro. Live aboard sailing was no longer on our agenda. While house shopping, we remained wary of spending money on restaurant meals. One afternoon in the center of a moderately trafficked Washington, DC business district, we needed to cook our not-ready-to-eat food. We parked next to the curb, set up the small propane stove and fried a steak. Awkward to be sure, but we saved the cash and enjoyed a healthy meal. Later we bought and remodeled a house within walking distance of Wayne's electrical engineering position and fifteen minutes from the Art League in Alexandria, Virginia. The DC museums were a twelve-minute drive.

I felt decadently rich with the income of an experienced engineer working for the DC Metro system. I hired a cleaner, Rosa, and her sister. This did not remain a business relationship very long. When her first-grade son had no school, and she thought she had to stay home with him, I told her to bring him with her, and we would play in my studio. He was great fun, and his creativity gratified my love of teaching. When I learned from Rosa that Raymond was failing first grade, that he was a misbehaved cut-up, I could not understand why. The school was reluctant to test him as there was a long line of English-speaking students needing evaluations by the school psychologist. When I learned he had not been taught any of the American classroom basics, I encouraged his mother to visit her family in El Salvador so he could be first evaluated by a Spanish-speaking psychologist. Our plan was if he had no academic disabilities, he should be taught to read in Spanish. With his confidence rebuilt, mother and son returned to states. I had my cleaner back on the job and Raymond quickly learned to read English. He became a star. The last I heard he was the lead in a play.

Our unusual relationship did not end there. Always looking for a new experience, I attended her church, sat in the women's section wearing a head covering, sang in Spanish, and bought an after-service meal. Before services, Rosa and friends would create savory Central American dishes in pots that would feed around sixty people. She sold these meals to the community at large and this increased church revenues.

Shortly thereafter, Rosa told me about a situation of one of the church's younger women. The woman was anticipating a wedding, but she no longer had a hymen, a rather serious problem in that community. Believing I was a doctor who knew everything and knowing she could trust me with embarrassingly sensitive information, she asked "What can we do? This marriage will not last if the groom finds out." My answer, "I will think about it," gave her hope. A few days later, I called Rosa with the name and address of a gynecological surgeon who would reinstate that symbolic hymen pro bono. They were on the bus to New York that week.

Rosa and I were not done with personal business. Several months later, she asked if I would take time to feel her breast. She had been worried for months, but being a private individual, she could not ask her husband or friends to examine her. She directed me to the area of concern and I said, "Rosa, this could be serious. You have a massive growth that cannot be ignored. It might be nothing, but you need be examined by someone who knows about these things."

"But I have no medical coverage," she said. "What can I do?" Again, it took a few days for me to find out what human research projects addressing breast cancer were seeking subjects. It didn't matter whether the treatment was chemical or surgical as she just wanted some avenue offering clarity and hope. She called the referrals I gave her and to our relief, she was eligible to participate in an intervention randomly assigned to her. Another win for all of us.

With Wayne now earning more income than I had ever touched, we had money to fly to Costa Rica and engage tour guides and modern eco cabins situated at the intersections of hot springs and rivers. Evening stars and colored lanterns enhanced these idyllic settings.

The day prior to our arrival in San Jose, the Volcan Poas had again scattered ash over houses, roads, windows, cars making it somewhat difficult to breathe. This was expected. We told our guide where we wanted to go. The Irazu Volcano, the tallest in the country, was our first choice. Others destinations were the cloud rainforests of Monteverde, and the Arenal volcano. I renamed them all as Blue Mountains. This was not correct, but it worked for me. As the only passengers in a van without springs, we felt our spinal discs crunching as we bumped along grossly pitted roads. We stopped at a butterfly farm, a bird sanctuary and marveled at rainforest spider monkeys. For us, these were almost boring tourist destinations, those typically advertised state side.

But then I knew there were hanging bridges and zip lines available. These could be definitely exciting. Given Wayne's fear of heights, I expected him to stay behind. However, he surprised me. He coolly announced his intention to be a full participant. This was in stark contrast to his history in asking me to always drive the Skyway Bridge in Florida or the New Zealand trip when he watched me climb down a gorge abandoning him and the car at the top. Now in Costa Rica, we again rented a car and gained access to the steep, rarely visited mountains. We ignored the insurance carrier's warning "Insurance will not cover death or damage on roads not on the map." We reasoned that since there were usually a few locals on those primitive roads, if they could survive, so could we.

Later, after strolling through the canopy in another of the national parks, we were both breathing hard. Bridges were essential to our upward climbs. We held onto rope railings with both hands. The bridges shook, they shuddered, and our hearts pounded. We felt the insecurity of older, wooden slated bridges. Then it was time for the piéce de résistance, the zip lines.

Zip lines are installed as shortcuts between separated, difficult-to-climb hills. Wooden platforms are installed at takeoff, and landings and cables are installed between the peaks. The zip line relies on the traveler's wearing a safety harness, leather gloves, and hand brake, technically called "a rider". This is a hand-controlled mechanism installed on the cable to which the rider's harness is attached. Upon jumping into the void, the adventurer relies on his or her own judgment regarding how fast he/she gains downhill momentum and when to slow down before ascending, without destroying him/herself on arrival at the next platform.

Wayne was okay with that first jump, but he choked as he approached the bottom of the catenary. His anticipation of the fast-flowing, white-crested currents indicating underlying boulders resulted in his abrupt, frightened overcompensation. He forcefully put on the hand brake, full stop. With his bum in the water, his body tied to a cable, and considerably distant from the second platform, we both wondered *what next? How do we get his 190-pound body out of this situation?*

The guide yelling reassurances counseled, "Tranquillo."

Fortunately, skinny and wiry does not abrogate strength, so hand over hand, our guide slowly hiked Wayne to his landing platform. The grinding, hard work of the Costa Rican did not allay Wayne's realization he was absolutely dependent on this stranger, a state of mind we both learned to tolerate as our physical disabilities increased during the coming years.

On returning to Virginia, I enjoyed the life of a full-time artist. Nonetheless I needed a friend, someone I could work with in my home studio, someone Wayne and I could cook for and someone who had shared interests. One New Year's Eve celebration found my new friend, Amanda, her husband, and Wayne arguing about Prince Hal in Shakespeare's Henry VIII. Wayne, the engineer, often a man of few words, shocked me with his capacity to quote extensively from the original text.

That January, my general MD upon completing my annual physical exam, unexpectedly referred me to the Washington Hospital Center. I could not believe that I, too, had a serious diagnosis— lymphoma. Illness is not a competitive sport, but this was an unusual coincidence. As a distinctive couple we were allowed concurrent his and her appointments. Each of us had our own specialist, but the entire team knew our background. They welcomed us as a couple, and we shared mutual admiration. Wayne always brought our caregivers candy.

Eventually, Wayne qualified for medical leave and took on the work of supervising my cooking and gardening. We took a holiday and flew to the Hilton in Tobago and Trinidad. Thus, we completed our goal of touring most of the Caribbean. We adapted to what was possible. I missed the adventure travel, the being up close and personal with locals, the sitting at pit fires listening to steel drums, but I reminded myself *What is, is good enough. Adapt.* We became connoisseurs of the best food. We accepted his and her massages. We carefully walked in clear water. Back home, the year he died, we (I) planted several hundred tulips and pruned pink and white magnolias.

Until his last year Wayne avoided talking about death. He did not pick up on my subtle hints that I might benefit from his buying additional life insurance. Not forcing the discussion, I gently prevailed. He bought a second $100,000 insurance policy. It was only during these last months that he willingly talked about burial plans. Now, acknowledging his increasing illness and the imminence of his death, he identified the thriving weeping cherry we had planted years earlier as the marker for his ashes. He had no interest in a cold, impervious granite headstone.

Cycling through critical care and near-death admissions, Wayne survived five years. Amanda, now an extremely close friend, and her son, Emerson, visited him in the hospital. At home, Emerson painted images of moving trains on two-by-ten-foot canvases. We hung these over the hospital curtains. Before Wayne died, Amanda told him, "Of all the men I have known, you are my best friend."

All too soon, my most intimate friend, my most extraordinary life partner, my husband, age fifty-two, died. The finality, the betrayal, overwhelmed me. Here I am sixty-seven. I am strong. I am kicking lymphoma into remission. And here he is— dead!

With grief beyond any I had ever known, I keened, I screamed, I cried for hours. I even tried pulling out my hair. This was not part of my plan. My intense mourning helped with my acceptance of this greatest loss. My mother's death twenty hours earlier was tolerable, but not his. Before driving to Ohio to honor the newly dead, I continued to keen in an unfamiliar voice. I swore. I yelled, immersed in the finality of his death. I raced through our home hanging yards of 50 inch wide black velvet from every window facing our street. I asked myself W*here did this velvet come from? Why did my artist supply closet contain black velvet?* Years earlier a flea market vendor had priced two uncut rolls of the velvet so low, I bought it, not knowing why.

Now I knew why. The undercurrents of pain and disease, realistic antecedents to my own death have always been a backdrop to my intense, joyful, colorful life. Visible body deterioration began in my early years with breast cancer. Other cancers, lymph, and skin were denied my total attention as other recurrent damage to my body required my compliance with other medical advisors. Two right knee surgeries of the ligament, first torn skiing in Aspen and prior to knowing Wayne, preceded a total knee replacement. Other surgeries, a 3-D spinal fusion, two hip replacements, and two rotator cuff replacements followed. Of course, a later diagnosis of progressive pulmonary fibrosis meant I would forever have difficulty breathing. It remains a recurring reminder of the eventuality of my own demise.

Physical pains are momentary diversions from my choices of how and where to savor what is. The uncontrollable flow, the undertow of pain and disease, reminds me of a flooding river eroding a thriving valley. It can strengthen, roar, destroy, change course, and then subside to a quiet stream. The undercurrent is omnipresent. This image firmly anchors and intensifies my respect and pleasure in the now. There is only the present. The past is past. The future is never predictable. I may as well enjoy my moments. They are all I have.

Chapter Fourteen

Single again, I asked myself *What's next?*
I craved another challenge, another mountain to climb.
Content in my remodeled Virginia home and truly
feeling integrated with friends, I knew this was not enough.
If I stayed, I would be on an all too boring downhill coast. I
believed my Long Island family could use help. Actually, I
needed them, but this would be hard for me to admit.

I bought a house because of its location on an acre of
woods sloping to the harbor and within a mile of Aaron's
family. I ignored the clouded, small windows, poor floor
plan, expensive taxes and non-functional AC and furnace.
As I happily squatted with Aaron on the roof of my new
home, I peeked between eighty-foot trees, trying to see the
harbor. Year round, the sparkle of water would be the most
I ever would see from my house, but then I did not have to
be greedy. I already had had years living on the water on
boats.

Painfully aware I had no income other than my social
security check and income from my savings, my first concern was to build revenue by creating a rental. Aaron, now
my contractor, agreed, and within months, that problem

was solved. We had designed and built an apartment in which I might be happy to live. Should I need increased income, I would rent the main house. I advertised the rental's enticements— quiet neighborhood, private blue stone patio on a heavily wooded hillside acre, fireplace, laundry room, large windows, queen sized bedroom, living room picture window, dishwasher, microwave, self-controlled heat, utilities included. The extra income rolled in following my advertisement and letting the apartment to a qualified applicant. Also, on the lower level, I anticipated re-establishing my art studio. Early on Aaron and I quickly set up the work-bench I had built in 1998 and my thirty-five-pound vise. He agreed to enlarge the garage windows, install twelve fluorescent lamps, an AC, a small gas heater and a slop sink. Later, I unpacked many other tools used to repair, problem-solve, and create gardens, paintings or sculptures. All the gear supporting other diverse interests found their place in close proximity—kayaking, hiking, camping, gardening, sewing, picture-framing.

Aaron's family was managing. It was not easy as there could never be a moment in which Cole was not under the watchful eye of an adult. The pediatrician referred the family to an early childhood developmental training program which clearly increased the strengths he has today. I waited. I told Aaron that when he and Diane were ready, I have had experience in accessing state programs to provide full-time care. They finally agreed the older children were not getting their fair share of attention and they were exhausted. They allowed me to initiate access to state care for Cole through the school system.

Aaron and Diane have remained the stable, bedrock of an extended family including three grandparents, several cousins, nieces and nephews. They are the ones who engender calm during the unexpected complications of life and admirably share their strength.

As Aaron worked on my house, he replaced the roof, rewired all the electricity, changed the leaking water pipes, installed larger windows and built a thirty-five-foot deck. I helped care for Cole, and documented his unaddressed educational needs. He did not understand danger, he would never talk, he did not sleep through the night, and he needed constant supervision. Aaron and Diane decided to apply for more appropriate help from the school and the state. Eventually Cole, one of two other Suffolk County residents in the last eighteen years, was funded for what would become full-time life care paid for by the state. In a country where we spend billions on military might, I believed Cole was also entitled and deserved twenty-four-hour supervision. My children also deserved support so they might better attend to their teenagers.

During these months, there was time for me to bond with Cole. Given his tentative beginnings, I believe we will always have a special bond. When we are with the family and he feels I am not attending to him, he will come behind me and clunk me on the head as if to say "Shape up. I'm here and don't you forget it." When visiting my house, he happily tears up old magazines as we look at and discuss the pictures. Food and boats are always his favorite subjects. He associates me with riding and then swimming off the family's trawler. He loves wearing his life jacket and following his dad digging clams. Of course, eating them is part of the outing. One vacation in Maine we canoed the shoreline. He was not content to sit in the canoe. With help, he grabbed onto a line and dog paddled alongside. I can definitely relate to this. Today Cole is sociable, likable, and happy. He knows who his family is and frets if we do not visit. He can use a simple computer to identify food he wants. He enjoys boating and traveling by auto. He likes to swim if the water is warm enough. He will always require twenty-four-hour supervision because he does not always recognize danger to himself and others. He cannot talk. We bring him home twice a month, and he lives on a campus three hours north.

As a new widow, I was again entrenched in Long Island, twenty-nine years after graduation. I had no local friends. I knew no one except my family. I was free to travel to places that had held little interest for Wayne. However, even though he was deceased, I intended he symbolically come along with me. We had the incomplete business of finishing his burial. I had not discussed with him my plan to put tablespoons of his ashes into zip lock baggies. My intention was he would mingle with the seas of the worlds as soon as possible. I needed the closure.

In La Jolla, California, I walked with Amanda along the cliffs late in the day. We found a place where his ashes could fall directly into the sea, and as the breeze took the ashes away from land, we watched a sailboat gradually traveling south along the horizon line. Like a movie, the boat's now red sails followed the sunset, and ever so gradually, we watched and watched until they disappeared, symbolically representing for us our loss. We both cried.

After a few weeks in La Jolla, I booked a ticket to Brisbane, where Wayne's entire family joined me on my mother-in-law's patio. The family and I reviewed fond memories and decided Wayne would be okay sharing space with his father under an olive tree. Afterward, Peggy, my favorite sister-in-law, and I, drove to Cairns and hired a captain and sailboat. Our day sail was initially calm, becoming rough in the afternoon, wherein I became queasy. My looming nausea was unpredictable, always dependent on the directions of winds and tide. Nature was against me, and I had to go up top and keep my eyes riveted to the coastline to prevent serious nausea. Ironically, Peggy, somewhat bored, went below deck to read. Without any difficulties, she chatted with the captain until we were returning to the marina. Then the captain let loose with vile, bigoted opinions about several aboriginals who were seeking admittance into a local bar. We watched the drama within forty feet of our slip and could hear the yelling, the cursing, and the mean-toned rejection the white men directed at the aboriginals, who remained quietly sober and hopeful customers. Of course, they finally had to go elsewhere, but the continuing rant of our captain really turned us off.

The next morning, Peggy and I flew to Darwin, my second trip. The first time I had traveled with Wayne, his brother Pete, and Peggy. We lived lavishly in the condo they owned, playing cards and dining in the town.

On this second trip, Peggy and I booked seven days in a newly constructed oasis complete with shading palms and rock-strewn brooks. We relished the modern cabins with air conditioning. Now, there would be sufficient time to walk the wharves, watch the unloading of international cargo ships, visit the cultural center displaying aboriginal art and gardens informing us of only some of what we were to see during the following weeks. Of course, there were what I considered the repulsive, omnipresent, glitter-filled shops selling nothing particularly original to the tourists.

However, I very much admired the idea of Darwin and its citizens, children of the initial colonialists and the aboriginals. Darwin had rebuilt itself after several cyclones that flattened the town. The locals did not give up their dreams to establish a base in this most northern part of the country. Their town and military site had even repelled attacks by the Japanese in World War I. Peggy and I emptied more of Wayne's ashes into The Timor Sea. Those ashes also remain part of the universe.

Darwin noticeably reinvents itself over centuries. The city remains for me another symbol of eternity because now I associate Wayne's memory with it.

During that trip, we booked a flight over Arnhem Land, the least developed area in the Northern Territory. West of the 4.3 million-acre Kakadu National Park, the flight allowed us to feel the power of another primitive, unmolested natural wonder. The sandstone escarpments seemed impenetrable, as did the rainforests, which created a canopy over the apparently unclimbable terrain. I had breathed deeply, but I would never be able to measure the immensity of the land unless I walked it, an unlikely goal. However, modifying my desire, Peggy and I rented a car. We were free to set our own agenda and cautiously explore a very small part of this World Heritage Site. The park was our objective, or more specifically, the 30 thousand BCE year old rock art galleries, more accurately described as caves. Without a timetable or the schedule of any of the many, comfortable, organized tours, we found the drawings using our own maps. The images on the walls of the caves embodied gods that sometimes appeared as if ancient X-ray machines had been used to increase the artists' extraordinary representations of bones and organs of those long deceased. One hunting scene was followed by images of other animals of those times. For example, there were drawings of the Tasmanian Tiger, including the stripes, and also a very long-necked turtle.

I happily admit that Kakadu has it all. To begin, six seasons predictably intertwine with the lifecycles of innumerable species, plants, and animals. Travelers are wise to avoid monsoon season. I recall Wayne telling me about a prior trip north, years earlier, when he felt like a prisoner. All the roads were closed for weeks. Other seasons include cooler, still humid-cold weather, or simply hot or dry. We were there during the cooler and still humid time.

Our Yellow Water River cruise gave us easy access to the Park's extensive diversity. Although our hikes allowed intimacy with the environment by touch and smell, the cruise reduced the likelihood of personal danger. We saw many saltwater crocodiles sleeping on top of each other and thriving undisturbed in the wetlands. We began to understand how the mangroves provided a protective barrier between the gulf and the mainland swamps. Near the wetlands, paperbark trees, sandwiched between gum trees and palms, shed two-foot strips of bark colored orange, tangerine, gold, and brown. The cruise guide directed our attention to specific animals and plants and because wattles seemed to me a funny word, I bothered to ask, "Are they important to humans?" The guide was quick to tell us the construction of most building (in rural areas) relies on this low-lying brush. Later, in a different time and place, I recognized wattles, packed with mud, forming the uprights and verticals of a small house grounded on a base of baked tiles.

Visits to small aboriginal settlements, isolated from the white population, helped me to understand how three hundred Bininji have survived at least 50 thousand years and continuously inhabit the land around Ubirr. This is one of hundreds of small clans surviving over tens of thousands of years. The clans speak hundreds of languages and their laws are particular to each group with the exception of verbal intergroup agreements. "The Law" of each clan is not written but retained through stories, their mythology, and song. The strongest personality is the accepted leader. Tribal rituals are secret, and it is only in the interest of money that the leaders will permit brief exposure of their original music, dance, and costumed performers. Body painting provides another mode to display historically linked artistry. Stories of the Rainbow Serpent, the creator, and the Lightening Man are told throughout in the country. Because these deities existed before the people, they remain the most honored.

Shortly thereafter, I returned to the states, enrolled in

university classes, continued gardening, and thought about what else I might do with my freedom. I visited several Florida friends Wayne and I had remained close to while we lived in Virginia. I met a fellow psychologist who had been a close friend prior to meeting Wayne. We might have dated, but he was already married. After Wayne died, he divorced his wife, and we were free to be romantic.

That did not work out and he subsequently courted another woman. It appeared we would remain very close friends forever. However, to my great disappointment, the new woman had a different strategy in setting up a serious relationship. My friend was allowed no further contact with me, not even by email or snail mail. Shocked and rejected, I suppressed my anger. *How could someone so much like me allow himself to be bullied into cutting off all close, prior female friendships?* The twenty-year friendship that had continued through both of our marriages was abruptly terminated. I attribute his compliance to her wishes was because he was really lonely and did want to risk losing her. Some things I cannot change. I continued to talk to and occasionally visit other Florida friends living in Tampa, Orlando, Port St. Lucie, and Ocala. Of course, whenever I was in Florida, I always spent time with my son Kurt and his family.

Although I didn't speak Spanish, I accepted an invitation from Amanda and our good friend Florenzio to rent an apartment and visit his extended family in Buenos Aries. Some of them were bilingual, especially the perceived patriarch, a retired teacher, whose wheelchair sustained his independence. However, I worried how he was going to get to our second floor rooms. No problem. Two nephews, familiar with the routine, carried him up the stairs faster than I could walk them. Florenzio had made empanadas with varied fillings, and we drank beer. There must have been twelve of us gathered in a noisy, joyous family reunion. Florenzio was a hero. His past as a union organizer in Paraguay brought him lifelong respect. He had often been involved in potentially violent demonstrations.

When his family arrived, he enthusiastically introduced us, Amanda, who spoke fluent Spanish, and Anita speaking a patois of broken Spanish, French, and English supplemented with dramatic hand gestures. The group said they understood me, but I know Amanda significantly helped with our ease in communicating. Some of the conversation turned to politics. Most of us shared similar values. We wanted everyone to have access to a good education, better job opportunities, medical care, and political representation with less corruption. They knew the names of the villains, and I understood their values.

Our Argentinian family gave us auto tours of Buenos Aires by day and night, and their pride in their high-towered buildings, universities, parks, and bridges was clearly displayed, because they would not suffer shortcuts to their planned tours. Sometimes, I just wanted to go home.

When Amanda and I decided to go to the dance halls that came alive after midnight, we joined mobs of youngsters waiting in lines following the sidewalk down the street. We were waiting admission to dance the tango, and Florenzio was our escort, allowing us to relax and enjoy the late-night energy. We always felt safe with him. He danced with reluctance, but he was a gentleman, and he complied when we asked.

Our reunion was much too short, but Amanda had to return to teaching in Washington, DC, and Florenzio had to manage his businesses, an electrical repair shop and a four-unit apartment building in Asuncion.

On my return to Long Island, I again returned to a life of learning at the university, gardening, and making friends, not really exciting, but good enough. However, I kept thinking about South America and realized I had never really spent time there. I had little knowledge of the cultures, the geography, the history. I decided to go, thinking *Language challenges be damned. This will be a first— new territory in my understanding of humanity.*

It was essential I go alone. Earlier I had learned from my experience on a Friendship Force group tour to Brazil, that I prized my independence more than being part of a formal, orchestrated group. During that trip, I felt our group leader automatically vetoed any suggestions I might make. For example, the Brazilian hosts liked my idea when I asked, "How would it be if we filled in unscheduled time with a stop at that cantina on the beach?" We could see beautiful, unbridled horses grazing nearby with a few teens playing soccer, and I knew water, sodas, or alcohol would be cheap. The American leader said, "No." She worried. "How would we pay for the drinks?" The Brazilians replied they were happy to take time to smell the sea, the flowers, and the horses. Consequently, our bus driver pulled onto the beach, and as my group disembarked, I described our revised plan. We would enjoy some unscheduled time at the cantina rather than in our rooms, and I would pay for any unpaid refreshments upon our departure.

Other experiences with that organized tour underscored my desire to travel to South America alone. For example, while traveling with the Friendship Force group, a rainforest guide did his best to expose us to the magnificence of a trail little used by people. I felt as if I were walking amidst cackling geese. It seemed the group could not let up on trampling the forest's feeble path and loudly discussing their grandchildren's latest achievements. I could not hear the silence. I found their lack of integration with the moment disturbing and asked the guide, "Can I walk thirty feet ahead so that I might no longer hear the geese?"

He smiled. He understood and said, "Go ahead, but

first, please watch me climb one of the tallest palm trees." I enjoyed his feat of endurance and strength and then walked happily ahead, as if I were the first explorer in this pristine territory.

Another reason I was convinced that in the future I needed to travel alone occurred when we were booked for a stay at an eco-hostel, four to a room. I knew I could not sleep with so much snoring, so I checked with the manager regarding the availability of a private room for an additional fee. He said "Yes," and was happy to make a few extra dollars.

My Friendship Force guide said, "No. You are not allowed to make any changes."

I asked, "Why?"

"Because I said so."

I said, "I am not your prisoner. Just watch me."

I slept well that night. Other petty power plays followed. I am happy to admit that at our last gala with the host families, I was enjoying dancing, sharing food, and making small talk with my favorite Brazilians. Between their skill in English, my energetic sign language and insufferable Portuguese, I received a memorable affirmation. In the style of a loving auntie, one woman patted my arm and said, "We think you are more Brazilian than all the rest. You really feel like one of us, and it's been a pleasure knowing you. You have offended no one." I really had fun with those Brazilians.

Before returning stateside, I again broke the rules by not flying home with the group. I booked a bus trip from Forteleza to Manaus, the gateway to the Amazon. Thwarted from a trip I had planned with my sister in the mid-1990s, I no longer needed to worry about out of control rain forest fires. The two-cabin boat gave me some closure to that unrealized experience. I spoke with isolated families along the river whose children went to school by canoe. I used gloves to throw night-jumping piranhas out of a dinghy. I spoke with a grandmother who had lived for seventy years in a primitive shelter built on the banks of the Amazon where the water ran quietly. Later, smothered by heat and the smell of diesel fuel powering us downstream, I saw the famous red and the black tributaries flow for miles side by side and finally converge into one color as they joined the Amazon. Although I knew I would have survived without an air-conditioned cabin on this small delivery boat, I recall how happy I was to enjoy the cool, bug-free environment each night.

Chapter Fifteen

Again, returning to my life in Long Island, I easily followed the past routine of visiting with family and friends, an occasional date, and attending lectures, working out at the gym, and gardening. I followed these planned activities as if they were a job. I knew I was still strong enough to travel alone, so rather than passive acceptance of time debilitating my body, I chose to see how else I might live on this planet before I died. I called Amanda and asked if she would like to spend a week in Panama with her friend Florenzio and me. The three of us made plans to share a first-class apartment. After she and I took occupancy, we learned with great disappointment, that he could not come. I told Amanda the three-bedroom apartment was beyond my budget, and I'd prefer downsizing to an inexpensive hostel. Although she would have preferred a more luxurious environment, my wonderful friend agreed, and we let a small basement room with one double bed and a dirty bathroom in a backpackers' hostel.

Roughing it, her apt description of life in the hostel, allowed access to a range of activities including traditional tourism and also, the unexpected, which for me was usually the greatest fun. The trip north on the Panama Canal included a review of Theodore Roosevelt's determination to connect two oceans and overcome ten years of construction and environmental obstacles. On board, our conversation with cattle ranchers from Idaho also proved informative. In their search for accessible and easy to import corn for their animals, they told a story that formed the basis of one of Amanda's teaching units once she returned stateside. Her students learned that some of the prime steaks they enjoyed in Washington DC may have been the result of the effectiveness of the Miraflores Locks and the distribution and survival of humans and cattle. The lesson easily incorporated use of mathematics, a study of cultural differences and the personality and politics of national leaders.

One evening upon returning to our hostel after an early evening meal, we were visiting with Marco, the guy at the front desk. Three gorgeous young women appeared, ready to depart into the poorly lit neighborhood. Charming and cute, they wore short halter dresses suggestively revealing legs and cleavage and clearly announcing their agenda. Marco suggested they might be wiser to wait until daylight. He could not guarantee their safety. Their enthusiasm for the night life prevailed. Looking forward to an unescorted night on the town, they departed. Twenty minutes later, they returned, with bruises, tears, torn dresses, and the loss of their pocketbooks.

Another morning, we asked Marco what we could do that was different from the activities of most tourists. He thought carefully and decided to tell us about the 365 San Blas Islands, just northeast of the isthmus to the canal. He spoke, as if sharing a secret, telling us the Guna tribe owned these islands and occupied only forty-nine. Two of the islands were designated for tourists. Those islands were designed to handle crowds of partying tourists who arrived in small trawlers. Marco described the loud bands which wildly played steady rhythms as the tourists drank from the abundant supply of margaritas and pina coladas. The tourists were easy prey as their clouded judgment loosened their caution and in addition to an abundance of alcohol, they also bought overpriced, "original" islander crafts. Marco stated this would definitely be something different for two pretty, single women. Hopefully we were kind when we told him we were not interested.

Then he came up with another "off the beaten path" suggestion. He cautiously said "I have friends, a three-generation family living alone on one of the islands. They might be interested in offering a place to sleep and breakfast for three nights. I think they might agree to a visit because you are teachers and definitely ladies. I think you and the children would enjoy each other and have a lot to share about your different lives."

We enthusiastically told him, "This is exactly what we are looking for."

Marco then said, "There are no telephone connections, but I will get a message to them, and if they are interested, they will provide transportation."

The grandfather of the family arranged to pick us up on a specific beach, in a dugout dinghy with an 8 HP frail looking engine. As we stepped over the gunwales, we learned his twelve-year-old grandson was in charge of bailing water and rowing with the two handmade wooden oars should the engine not have sufficient power.

As we gained purchase over the incoming tide, we realized we were losing ground because the northern winds increased the height of the waves which were flooding our small boat. We and our backpacks were soaked. All of Amanda's technical equipment— phone, camera, computer, ostensibly protected in zip lock baggies—were destroyed. We breathed hard as we watched water rising to nine inches in what appeared to be a foundering boat. This striking change in our mode of transportation underscored that we were on our way to a genuinely alternative way of living. On the way, despite the drama, grandpa even managed to catch a fish for dinner.

Upon our arrival, we followed the mother and the two children to our room—an eighteen-foot, roofless circular corral constructed with bamboo, no nails or hooks on which to hang clothes. We were pleased the two hammocks, although not particularly clean, were hung within talking distance so that later, when lying in them, we could read to each other stories and poems I had carried under my foul weather gear. We felt comfortable and appreciated our exposure to a different kind of luxury.

We were shown "the toilet", about forty feet from our corral. This amazing contrivance consisted of a toilet bowl banked by sand and enclosed with bamboo screening. An eighteen-foot ladder barely reached the platform where a ten-gallon tank could be filled with water by the father. The amenities of "a flush toilet" were another kind of luxury because we did not have to dig holes for our waste.

Amanda asked, "What do we do in the middle of the night?" I laughed. "Well, you see that palm tree? Either its leaves, or if you're lucky, the clouds in the night sky will cast a shadow. If you move quickly, there will be time to squat in those shadows. If there are no shadows, you will have to squat anyway and be done with it."

Much of our time was spent with the children. They loved us, and we became their entertainment, creating language and card games. The four of us had fun correcting each other and practiced both English and Spanish as we dramatically told stories. Sometimes either Amanda or I explored the island alone and learned we could walk the entire shoreline in a few hours. Afterward, we talked about the quietness of our walks, despite the sounds of the waves and birds, and sadly recognized that all the pristine shores of the world might now be covered with endless tons of plastic debris, foam, bags, and bottles. We could talk about the self-centeredness of other humans. It was difficult to admit we were part of the problem.

Meals were always a luxury as there were no in between snacks. Our first meal on that San Blas island triggered more drama when later, we returned to Panama City. The family had butchered a chicken, and Grandpa had cooked the chicken and the fish on an open fire. He used a wooden cutting board to cut meat, fish, and vegetables. After a few meals, we noticed the food, minus exotic spices was always delicious and we were hungry. We did not notice the bacteria.

About the time we returned to the beach from where we first embarked, Amanda became violently ill with uncontrollable bowel activity. She walked as far as she could from the landing site before cramps overwhelmed her, and although there were people around us and watching, she squatted. We made it to our hostel without further incident, and just in time for me to share her symptoms. For twenty-four hours we competed for use of the one commode, the tub, and space on the filthy broken tiled floor. We puked. We emptied our bowels of all fluids. We knew we had fevers. Dressed in fouled undergarments, we sweated and shivered. Sometimes both of us made it into our now filthy double bed, and then, despite the extreme cramping, we laughed, asking ourselves, "If this is not intimacy, what is?" As friends in the states, we had enjoyed reading plays in our living rooms or visiting cultural events or cooking wonderful meals. This was a very different kind of togetherness.

Because we were not getting better, and Amanda could speak fluent Spanish, we decided she would ask the new night clerk for help in ordering a taxi. An hour later, none had arrived. Unremitting pain continued as she, increasingly weak, returned to our bed. I then dragged myself to the front desk.

I screamed, "Urgencia," dramatic and to the point. "Urgencia." "Necesito." "Hospital." "Taxi." Despite my broken Spanish, each word was loud and distinctive. That clerk would understand, or if he did not get the message, I intended to lie down at the hostel's front entrance, wrapped in my makeshift cover-up, a bed sheet. In ten minutes, a taxi arrived.

Now ready to leave our room, Amanda asked, "What do I do if I have to go— in transit?'

I said "Take a plastic bag. If that doesn't work, it's the best we can do."

Emergency Room staff transferred us from the cab to two gurneys and rolled us into an unexpectedly quiet and modern facility. We wondered *Are we the only patients?* The MD and nurses quickly transferred us to our beds, covered us with luxurious clean sheets despite our smelly bodies, and started IVs for hydration. Blood was drawn, lab analyses were initiated, and medicines for the painful bacterial infection were administered at the hospital. We each paid $152.17 to the Hospital Nacional and were discharged. Our departure felt cool and efficient.

Shown the exit at four in the morning, we walked out the doors to the sandstone steps. No taxis were on the street. I wondered why no one in the hospital had offered to help us in finding one. Sitting on those cold, uncomfortable steps, we waited and waited in the dark. Hospital lights glittered gray shadows on Amanda's face and I blamed myself for what had happened to her.

Our instructions were to go to the people's clinic in our neighborhood the next morning because Amanda needed more laboratory analyses. Her infection was more serious than mine. Upon entering the clinic, we were awed by the numbers of mothers holding infants and many children crying. It seemed the entire community was lined up on folding chairs lining the perimeter of the room, and there were puddles of water everywhere. In the bathroom, water flowed from a faucet that flooded the laundry type sink. It puddled onto the floor and into some of the stalls. The clinic was a sanitation disaster.

Fortunately, Amanda was seen by a mature, caring bilingual MD who had trained in the states. She would follow through on a further evaluation of Amanda to assure she was being given the best medication appropriate for her illness. All of us were aware my flight south was scheduled for the next day. Amanda's flight was two days hence. The doctor assured me she would telephone Amanda at the hostel and instruct her regarding further treatments.

I left the next day.

Amanda knew that after our time in Panama I had planned to fly to Ushuaia, Argentina, the southernmost city in the world. I knew little about the country, so this appeared to me as good a destination as any other, and with a one-way ticket, my future was open. I carried maps and one travel guide representing all the countries of South America. I knew little about the continent, but that was part of the adventure. I would be stepping into the unknown not trusting credit cards and ATM's. On previous trips I had had technical problems with credit cards and travelers cheques. This time I intended to be independent of non-performing machinery. I believed cash trumps credit cards, checks, money orders, and wire transfers. Consequently, I traveled with thousands of dollars in cash sewn into shirt collars and hems, folded into Wite-Out bottles, eyeglass, and contact lens cases, rolled into lipstick cases, pen covers, Blistex tubes, and rouge pots. On a green 3x5 index card, I had carefully listed the number of one hundred-dollar bills hidden in each container. I did not travel with a camera or phone. I wore twenty-dollar earrings and alternated between one pair of pants, one skirt, three changes of underwear (no bra), four shirts, and one rain jacket.

Amanda was still quite ill when I left her. My ticket was not refundable, and she had her ticket to Washington D.C. She was waiting for a summary of her labs. Having been in Mexico prior to meeting me in Panama, she not only had a bacterial infection attributed to our meals in San Blas, but also from food she had eaten in Mexico.

I did not know how worried she was about me. Later, she told me she believed I was planning my last hurrah and probably keeping an impending death secret. Fortunately, this was not the case. I left her without any future address or way she or my family could contact me. In an attempt to diminish their worry, I would say "Either I would have no problems and enjoy the experience, or, if I got sick or had an accident, someone would help me. If no one helped, I would either live through the problem, possibly suffer and get better or die. This happens to millions each day and I will always be part of that life-to-death cycle.

Restless, I knew it was time to move on. Before I did, I wanted to rethink why I was traveling through South America with an unconsidered, apparently random plan.

Upon reflection, this was not the case. I listed five reasons—unusual settings in which to read great literature reflecting the counties I was visiting, a lack of a mate, a need for some independence from groups, a need for a totally new experience, and then my closeted arrogance of a need for bragging rights.

For me the process of cutting loose was important. The reality of possible danger, pain, and other losses paled with my anticipation of the future of relatively unscripted months.

In 2007, Ushuaia, Chile, was still a small town with little traffic. I walked the hills to a newly constructed back-packers' center, and I was quite pleased with the modern plumbing. I walked everywhere, so on a steep, downhill walk, I came to the town's only museum that housed a simple display of local aboriginal history. As I looked at the photos of estancias named after Europeans, I again realized these extensive ranches of sheep and cattle existed only because of the work of the aboriginals. The museum's few photos supported images of harsh survival in a challenging environment with pictures of workers crowded in large dormitories and primitive kitchens. The museum displayed journal notes written by a priest who described hundreds of natives dying of the diseases the settlers had imported along with their guns and visions of wealth.

Later, I walked to the docks and unexpectedly found a cruise scheduled to visit a few islands in the archipelago. I smiled when I disembarked and found myself amidst an enormous penguin colony that the captain told me gathered annually at this specific island during breeding season. The flightless birds, upon swimming out of the sea, begin their noisy calls to find their prior mates. As serial monogamists, they share in the care of the eggs, the feeding of the fledglings, and the protecting of the nest. I continued to smile as I observed them waddling shoulder to shoulder with feathers resembling suits. Except for breeding season, they are always in the water and self sufficiently swim the seas.

I distributed more of Wayne's ashes in the Antarctic Ocean.

My pleasure in my coursework of the 1980s influenced my desire to spend time in South America and many of the activities I finally chose, once there. I carried some of the Central and South American modern classics not yet knowing which country was the homeland of each writer. I intended to read these poems, novels, or essays and learn a little about the lives of these writers. I wanted to visit their homes, but they were not always easy to locate.

In Ushuaia, I began to orient myself and reduce some

of my confusion about where I was and what was geographically significant. I had not prepared by learning about that continent's history or geography. By immersing myself in unfamiliar circumstances, cultures, and places, I learned in the moment and voraciously absorbed all that seemed relevant in that moment. I asked many questions, continuing to recognize that the past, the present, and the future are one. There is always more than is immediately visible.

Geography has determined much of history, and after I finally figured out that the Andes are the longest mountain range in the world, beginning in northern Venezuela and dropping to the sea in the province of Tierra del Fuego, some of the stories I knew began to make sense. Tierra del Fuego, translated "Land of Fire," refers to indigenous fires Captain Cook had recorded on his passing through the strait, not volcanoes. Before the trip, I had not known what an archipelago was. During my travels, the term appeared everywhere, and I came to understand how important the relatively easy accessibility of the islands and mainland ports determined the changing cultures.

As I left Argentina, I began my bus trek up the western coast of Chile, which was easier than walking, but still seriously fatiguing. The buses stopped at what I might label nondescript ports and settlements. They mostly served the indigenous folks, who dressed in colorful clothing that reflected their tribal heritage. Getting off those hard-used buses, I was happy to stretch my legs and walk about the towns. Cold, biting winds did not deter me from mindfully entering a maze of beauty and geographic drama where, if I had traveled far enough, I might have counted hundreds of snow-capped mountains, each more than 13,000 feet and named on the postcards sold in the shops. All of those photos paled compared to what I really saw. The awe I felt during this passage instilled deeply carved images and feelings into my memory. To date, other visions of beauty and drama have not exceeded the effect of Patagonia.

Taking the bus, I made my first stop, Puerto Arenas, the largest of the two international ports in Chile. As expected, it had a larger population than the other towns. I happily walked about this and subsequent smaller towns on my way north. Occasionally, I stayed overnight and was not distracted by the sudden temperature changes.

Uneventful stops in Puerto Natales and Puerto Montt offered no clues to the adventures I was about to have in Temuco, a town located one-third of the distance to Santiago.

I had rented a room in a two-story, three-bedroom colonial furnished with heavy wooden European-style furniture. I was almost too comfortable because the owner of the bed and breakfast would provide my meals upon request. Craving a little excitement, I walked into town, looking for a tour guide/travel agent. I remarked on my good fortune when I quickly located a rafting group departing the next day. I was one of six rafters and two guides who drove an hour inland and then dragged our raft into the river, reportedly Class II to IV difficulty. I did not anticipate going overboard because the river was relatively low at this time of year. Nevertheless I was grateful that helmets and life-jackets were required. I had known the danger of rocks during canoeing and rafting in Missouri, New Jersey, and Wyoming. My five teammates were twenty to thirty-years-old and provided strength I did not have. The guides, always on the lookout for unexpected rapids or swiftly changing channels took turns yelling "hard right" or "hard left" loud enough so the rest of us could hear them over the crashing currents of the river.

We paddled hard when they told to do so, and we followed their directions as best we could or, we might suddenly find ourselves flipped into the icy water. Later,

we saw other guides rescuing other rafters who, to save
themselves, held onto rocks or were unsuccessfully trying
to swim to shore. As we moved through one rock tunnel
with a six-inch clearance, I was especially thankful for my
helmet. With waves and currents forcefully changing water
levels, I actually, to my surprise hit my head. It really hurt.
My neck hurt, but I was okay. It certainly paid to have an
outfitter during that trip.

The guides pulled onto shore and announced that they
would take care of the raft as we needed to climb the hill in
front of us. We obediently got out, and making our way up
a twenty-foot, somewhat slippery, forty-five degree slope
of granite boulders, we enjoyed a few minutes of smelling
the pine trees and catching our breath. Then, without preparing us for this challenge, the guys told us to jump off a
horizontal rock about twenty-five feet above relatively
quiet, deep water while they waited below. As I write this, I
am laughing because, at that moment, we just looked at
each other. No one, not even the guys, offered to go first,
and the women, now reverting to "girly" girls, said absolutely "No way." We waited for one of us to volunteer. The
guides below encouraged us. No one responded.

I had jumped off high diving boards before, so trusting
and impatient to get on with life, I walked to the edge and
jumped. The rest of my group followed, and we all climbed
into the waiting raft.

When we arrived at out final landing, we engaged in a
celebratory farewell, and it occurred to me that this was my
seventieth birthday. I shared that information with the
others. My team stood on the pontoons holding their pad-
dles in the air and sang. They wanted me to join them bal-
ancing on the pontoons, but I knew better. Exhausted, I
kept myself firmly standing on the floor of the raft with my
paddle serving as a walking stick. I still remember my fatigue as we returned to our van.

A few days later, I appeared to have slept through a fairly serious earthquake because upon awakening I could see the windows were not exactly aligned, and there were slight cracks in the plaster. As I walked down the curved stairs holding onto the varnished railing, I became more aware of the strength of the earthquake as the clerestory was broken and a few half inch floor to ceiling cracks scarred the recently painted walls. When I entered the breakfast room, I noticed the murals of idyllic European parks and well-dressed eighteenth century families picnicking and felt comforted and safe. I sat down at one of the two tables placed next to each other, one set for a couple and one for me.

Areles and William were excited about the earthquake, reporting to me that the entire infrastructure of Temuco was down and would not return to normal for more than a week. College students whose parents lived in Santiago, they had planned to drive their car to a nearby lake where they had rented an off-season, two-bedroom cabin. They invited me to join them not expecting me to underwrite their costs. Areles gave me a heads-up when she stated there were no extra sheets or towels, but I was quite welcome to one of four bunks in the second bedroom. Within minutes, while eating our hard-boiled eggs, tomato, perfectly ripened avocados, toast with marmalade and drinking freshly brewed coffee, I happily accepted their offer. I sensed they appreciated having an English-speaking friend during their summer break. William would be returning to the states to work on ski lifts in Colorado, and Areles was looking forward to joining her uncle in China where she would work in his manufacturing company.

Chapter Sixteen

We quickly packed and went to the shops to buy food for the week. Fortunately, my new friends had already purchased some provisions because the markets had no refrigeration, lights, nor operating cash registers. People with cell phones had not yet located generators to assist in recharging their batteries. Within two hours, we had taken the back roads to a lake bordered by a half dozen unoccupied cabins. We unloaded the car, and I understood I would have to use the clothes in my pack to serve as towel, pillow, and blanket. However, given my history, I was not exactly roughing it.

We easily fell into our self-assigned chores. Areles and I were quick to manage the kitchen and enjoyed the process of speaking in Spanish and English. I humbly admit we created unusual food combinations given our haphazard assortment of canned vegetables and rice, but we enjoyed what we had. William was in charge of the grill (before the fresh meat ran out) and our nightly pisco sours, which he served each evening on the deck. He also brought pisco sours to us as we cooked. He had built a fire pit near the shoreline to provide atmosphere for later evening conversations as we enjoyed the stars in the sky, the sounds of crickets and frogs, and the occasional fish splashing. Not one of us spoke about the earthquake. We were living in the moment of what was good in that cabin by that lake.

Toward the end of the week, we had noticed the lack of anyone in the other cabins, and William had noted that the pontoon boats were unchained. He conspired with us to help him drag a paddle pontoon boat into the lake. We climbed aboard and paddled away with minimal guilt. After all, we were not stealing it.

On our return to our bit of shoreline a big man stood, angrily shouting, and I felt the bottom drop out of my stomach. We were undeniably guilty. William, with great confidence or should I say bravado, said, "I'll take care of this." He waded through knee-deep water toward the angry stranger, intending to make a quick peace. Allowing the angry owner of the pontoon to rage, William brought closure to the event when he offered an extravagant rental fee to the owner, and we returned the boat to the storage area.

That evening under the stars, we toasted marshmallows at the pit-fire and drank more pisco. I truly enjoyed my friends rationalizing our incredible criminal activity.

As I dreamily watched the fire, I imagined my children reading the front page of a Temuco newspaper. I felt their shock as they realized there was a photo of their mother wearing her bikini and standing pitifully next to the pontoon boat. The headline stated "Seventy-year-old grandmother arrested for boat theft." I imagined my children wrestling with the question they asked themselves *Should we laugh or cry?* I never knew their reaction as I never told them.

Instead of parting company at the end of the week, my friends invited me to ride with them to Santiago to meet Areles's family and William's landlady. In my mind, this was the way to travel and genuinely learn about others.

Upon our arrival in this beautiful, but intimidatingly large city, I was grateful William took charge of my safety. He ruled out several B&Bs, and selected a private home occupied by the owners and managed by their son. The environment felt genteel with silver utensils and a beautifully set breakfast table.

They told me where reasonable meals could be purchased and which direction to walk on the tree-lined street to access the bus system. Each day, I passed the music institute seeing students smoking and hanging out on the steps. I could hear a variety of squeaky sounds coming from the interior. In a short time, my acquaintance with Señora Ramirez, the owner of my residence, became a friendship. We took buses to concerts in the cultural center and walked in botanical parks. Our conversations were limited, but sufficient to share information about our families, our work and what we liked to do with free time.

Areles's mother was kind enough to honor my visit with a celebratory family dinner. She served us using her fine china, sterling silver, and crystal stemware. She had prepared a roast. Areles's grandmother, father, and two younger siblings eagerly asked me many questions about my family and life in the states. I reciprocated by asking an equal amount of questions about their lives. Areles's father was an architect, rather silent by nature, but definitely reaching out to me when he showed me photos of some of his buildings.

My bizarre encounter with William's elderly landlady revealed her fear I would be staying overnight and take advantage of her "William." She repeatedly opened his door to ask, "Do you need anything?"

I noted his small, poorly-lit bedroom had a small closet, a bed, a table, and a chair. I could see that a hotplate and a refrigerator completed these basic accommodations. I understood none of this was important to William because he was a carefree, fun-loving student with little interest in homemaking. When we said our goodbyes, he promised to visit me on Long Island after ski season. As I expected, he did not follow through on my invitation. I was okay with his consistency in non-commitment.

I came to know Santiago by walking. Thousands of trees, planted centuries ago, had grown to create canopies and dense green zones with gardens and small lakes. Although Santiago is a city with four-lane boulevards, I usually chose to walk. The greenery beckoned me and kept me moving. The trees were an attraction with roots intruding on the sidewalks and sometimes looked like the legs of elephants. The only ones I recognized were the lindens and cherry trees. Later, I learned the ones with the enormous roots were probably ombu.

One afternoon, I planned to attend a political rally outside a fifteen-story government building. As I was waiting for the speaker to climb to the platform, hundreds of well-dressed men and women flooded from the building, walking quickly, shuffling, crowding me and the audience. Everyone seemed tense, and everyone was talking. Finally, I surmised an earthquake was imminent.

The earthquake arrived, the ground shook, a politician gave a speech and government workers returned to their offices.

Another, larger earthquake occurred two days later, flipping sidewalks to their vertical axis and frustrating me after a long, hot walk to a major city park. The park appeared to be mostly a monolithic rock, but after being refused access, I could see the huge, structural cracks. I walked onward, anticipating I would spend the rest of my day in a cool, noteworthy museum. Again, I was blocked. On arrival, I had difficulty believing 20 percent of the building had cleanly split from the whole and was lying in

broken heaps. These earthquakes were certainly an inconvenience.

I booked a bus tour from Santiago to Valpraiso. My
goal was to visit Pablo Neruda's oceanside house and learn
more about the man who wrote romantic poetry and became an international diplomat. Neruda's evolution from
tender, lonely, impoverished, rejected poet to his election
as a senator in the communist party and a confidante to the
socialist President Allende is inspirational. The house reflected Neruda's humor, interest in nautical art, and the
influence of a woman who knitted the bedspread. Important
to me was his capacity for revealing the depths of his own
feelings in poetry and concurrently giving of himself to improve the lives of millions in political speeches and articles.

The day before I departed to Lima, Areles, William,
and I planned a late afternoon picnic on Cerro San Cristo-
bal. The forty-five foot statue of the Immaculate Concep-
tion cast a feeling of protection over the city, especially at
night when its lights shined into the valley below. The
snow-capped mountains were no longer visible as a feeling
of quiet descended the hill. We shared a bottle of wine from
a Mendoza vineyard, a welcome change from William's
pisco sours, and said our goodbyes.

Before leaving Santiago, I answered an ad and booked
a week in a single room on the floor above a music store in
Lima. The price was more than reasonable. Upon arriving, I
applied my system of writing the address of my destination
on a 3x5 card, which I would then give to the taxi driver. I
engaged a cab at the bus terminal. Entering the store, I was
welcomed by the manager and led up the creaky, worn,
wooden steps to a small, circular hallway accommodating
two heavily locked wooden doors. Upon entering my room,
I paused to watch cockroaches scuttle in the galley. Since
bedbugs were not visible, it was rather late, and I was definitely tired, I said goodnight and locked my door. Taking a

much-needed shower I quietly yelped when a cockroach tickled my palm as I grabbed the bar of soap. In the morning, I easily decided to leave this place without a plan or any information about possible rooms to rent. I did not have the energy to ask for a refund, but more important, I was well aware that a substandard room was better than none. I did think I might come back later to get my money.

Stepping out the door at ground level, I put on my hat, hitched up my trousers, slung one heavy sack over my left shoulder, and tightly gripped the other bag with my right hand. I knew I would miss the sounds of tango and salsa as the loudspeakers never stopped announcing the presence of the shop. However, more important was my need to find a safer, cleaner accommodation. Temperatures were in the mid 90s (Farenheit) and I was seriously sweating as I walked towards the city-center. I walked slowly, one foot in front of the other, mostly looking at the sidewalk to avoid falling and occasionally looking upward to avoid running into an obstacle or missing signs indicating room rentals. After what seemed like the end of my endurance, the temperature seemed more agreeable. The street was now lined with shade trees. I continued walking, and as I looked downward, there appeared golden grates and then stripes of gold leading me to tall, double doors with twelve-inch vertical gold-covered door handles. *Am I hallucinating?* I asked myself. *Impossible. Not my style* I told myself.

In front of me, two well-groomed hotel clerks, wearing jackets with their names and the name of the hotel sewn onto their pockets, welcomed me. Upon my revelation of how urgently I needed a place to stay and that I was quite fatigued, I caught my breath. Then I added that I loved the luxury and ambiance of their hotel, but I required a referral to a more affordable place. These young men thoughtfully replied that first, their mid-week rates were not terribly expensive and second, I could check my bags with them and walk two blocks to the locoturio. I asked what that was, and they explained it was a commercial telephone center, and if I made the call from outside the hotel, the rate would be even less. This I did, again stressed by the unknown communication challenges. The call went through. The price was manageable. And I returned to the hotel with a reservation.

The busboy carried my bags, and we took the elevator to my third-floor room. Astonished with the luxury of the room, I first considered its furnishings. Definitely designed in the style of art nouveau, the choice and placement of the furniture revealed the artistry of a professional. The arm of the white suede chaise lounge was in the waterfall style. The camel back of the two-person sofa was also white suede, a place much too elegant and clean for me to place my dirty, worn, travel bags. Gold plate adorned the over-sized bathroom fixtures. Of course, the white linens were thick and soft as the bathrobe.

My view from the French door allowed me to look over the green canopy of trees and I could easily see the small tables carefully placed under awnings ready for after-noon tea. I picked one, went downstairs and soon was en-joying that luxury. Somehow, I connected with a nurse and her two friends living in Lima because they could obtain college degrees there with little expense. They shared an apartment, and one had a father my age who had just ar-rived from Texas. The four were planning a trip to Cuzco and the Inca ruins which were also on my agenda.

Considering our shared travel agenda, we agreed to meet the next afternoon on the top floor of another swanky hotel for drinks. The young women, especially the one with the father, suggested that we older folk share a room. Rooms were not easily available and very expensive. After a week of nurturing myself and being nurtured by others, I had paid for a massage and gourmet food, I was now ready to travel to Cuzco and take the train to Machu Picchu. I understood that the railroad station in Cuzco was extremely crowded and notorious for pickpockets and bag slashers. Considering my lack of fluency in Spanish and then the danger, I found the offer of the young women, who did not quite know what to do with the sixty-five-year-old visiting father, quite appealing. I accepted.

The students had booked a room for themselves prior to the father's arrival, but they managed to locate a small, ground-level room for the two of us. Outside our small window, the Texan and I could hear tourists from many countries chatting as they walked by on the sidewalk. Even more intrusive, the foul odors were so rank that I held my nose each time I entered the room. My roommate and I never did figure out if the smell was coming from the seal on the toilet, or the drain of the shower, or possibly the water trickling down the street along the curb. Given the shortage of affordable rooms, we did not complain. Eventually we got used to the stench.

The Texan was not talkative but he was considerate in sharing the bathroom and allowing me privacy when needed. I most appreciated his willingness to walk with me to see some of the sights. Navigating the streets was challenging. The alleys followed paths initially created by Incas in the 1500s. Cautiously, I maneuvered unexpected steepness, uneven cobblestones, and people going in the opposite direction on sidewalks wide enough for one. As we walked single file, I held onto the Texan's hand to avoid stumbling into traffic.

After a day immersed in the ruins of Machu Picchu, I could appreciate the intense, spiritual experience recorded by thousands of visitors. Initially built as a retreat for an Inca Emperor, Machu Picchu became the place for festivals and religious ceremonies. Archaeologists initiated serious exploration in 1911 and by 1983 100 million internet users selected it as one of the seven wonders of the modern world. Earthquakes have twice leveled Lima and Cuzco, but not Machu Picchu. Within one hundred years the Inca had created one of the world's largest empires only to succumb to the wars and diseases brought by the conquistadores. Their engineers created this aesthetic and technical wonder without motors, wheels or metal tools. They polished stones to fit so tightly that during earthquakes the stones appear to bounce. After a quake stops, then and today, the stones drop back into position. Never discovered by the conquistadores, it remains a symbol of the apogee of the Inca Empire.

I said my goodbyes and thanked my friends for their care and support. I had decided to take a local bus west through the Sacred Valley because I wanted to know more about the valley that supported the craftsmen who built Machu Picchu. I wondered about the early inhabitants who settled around the river, built terraces for crops, and grew abundant fields of maize and other foods. The strength of the empire was not only because of gifted warriors, engineers, and craftsman. It rested firmly on those who supplied them food, managed the cattle, wove their clothing, and cared for the families of the builders. I believe the valley, nestled between two rivers and steep hills, was most likely dominated by women. I was pleased to spend the night with a family in a humble guest house at the end of the line and then returned to Lima where I had rented a room let by a single mother, the divorced daughter of a deceased father. She introduced me to her other renter, Debra, a post doc who had been awarded a grant to document rural, not commercialized, artisan weaving in Russia, Peru, and Guatemala. We three hit it off immediately, and although the owner of our house was often busy with her indulged five-year-old, we sometimes attended artisan fairs together.

Even today, the owner remains a sponsor of women weavers near Lima with the goal of increasing their income. In contrast, Debra grew up in a house with her bedroom overlooking the San Francisco Bay. As a Fulbright scholar, she had income, which gave her unfettered freedom to follow her interests. Together we visited settlements not always on the map. We took a side trip to explore the erotic museum, which was unlike anything I had encountered in the United States.

My alertness immediately increased as Debra and I departed a tour bus which had delivered us, at eight o'clock one night to a distribution center for "hand-woven" sweaters. When we stepped off the bus in a solid drizzle, we were instructed to climb perhaps thirty tiered steps, without a railing. Because I did not carry a walking stick or an umbrella, I held on to Debra. The dark and thick wooded land to my right and left increased my wariness. The courtyard beyond the steps was probably delightful during daylight, but at this hour, the only light I could see emanated from a more than two-story, barn-like structure with struts and lofts. This light reflected on wet, uneven, smooth rock sufficiently uneven to create puddles little children might enjoy, but not for me at that time and place.

The interior of the barn, not filled with hundreds of "hand-woven", but rather commercially-pressed and color coordinated sweaters disappointed us. A token collection of truly hand-woven sweaters was present, but lost in this mire of commercialism. Those tourists, thrilled by the low prices, would probably not know the difference on their return home. They had paid for bragging rights.

Another day Debra and I took a taxi to a private museum located in a deceased mine owner's home. Access was "by appointment only." Debra had learned about the museum through friends of her parents. Upon our arrival, the heavily bolted door was unlocked by the son of a deceased successful gold miner who eventually created a collection of solid gold artifacts. Musty rooms with huge and heavy display cases, and life-size sculptures crowded our passage throughout the house. It was definitely a museum. The abundance of gold dishes and goblets, religious items, and jewelry became, for me, almost boring. I was more interested in the son's quality of life. His skin was sallow. He was thin. He did not smile. He said little, and he appeared, to me, to be depressed. He had inherited the burden of living with and guarding the gold with a prohibition of not giving the collection to a museum or selling it piece by piece. When I left, I felt sorry for him.

I returned to my room in Lima without further plans and realized I had no interest in traveling onto Ecuador and the Galapagos. I was tired and wanted to go home. I started the booking process using the room telephone around eleven o'clock that night and immediately encountered difficulty. The airline clerk could not understand that I could be an American without a round trip ticket. Finally convincing her after she vetted me asking many, many questions, I charged a ticket from Lima to Texas and then onto New York, the quickest way home. Arriving at JFK around 3am the following day, I was very uncomfortable. All the shops were closed. The halls were void of people. I could not see even one porter. Fatigued with the weight of now heavy luggage, I missed the travel advisors who normally stood at their counters. I stopped in the middle of the huge exit hall and told myself, *Take a deep breath. You can do this. Think.* I was about to cry because I had no coins to make a pay-phone call for a limousine driver when a floor sweeper magically appeared.

"Do you have change?" I asked.

He reached in his pockets, and gave me a handful of change for my dollar. I connected with a limousine service and relaxed during the drive to Centerport, Long Island.

As I opened my front door with the key I carefully kept accessible in my wallet, I was pleased to see the LED post light bulbs still working. The lamps glowed circles of soft, golden light over the many plants I had transferred from Virginia. I breathed deeply the smell of damp night odors emerging from my woods and listened to crickets chirping. I was home.

Chapter Seventeen

The next day I notified family that I was home and would see them when they were available. I quickly returned to my normal schedule of activities. I rejoined my gym, showing up three to five times a week. I signed up for courses at the university, attended discussion groups at the libraries, and eventually created two women's groups. One meets at my house for lunch and great conversations. The other at a restaurant. I continued to talk with Amanda and sometimes we travel to each other's homes so we might have extended time with each other.

I joined a yacht club, hoping to get back on the water as someone's guest. The commodore invited me to join a Thursday night sailing group during the summer months. This remains a consistent pleasure except when illness impairs me to the extent I cannot climb onto the boat. Some of the original group are now trained to be crew on his racing team, and I am somewhat envious because these last few years I can no longer turn heavy winches or manage deck work or hang ropes over pilings. However, I am diligent about bringing food. I know I would be a handicap if I tried to race.

To compensate for my increasing weakness because of back surgery, a knee replacement, and later two hip replacements, I bought an ultra-light kayak that I could independently load onto and off the roof of my car. I now can pack camping equipment, food, water, a tent, a stove, and an icebox in my new Outback. A single-width foam mattress, laid out the length the car, allows me to sleep wherever and whenever I become tired. Traveling with the kayak somewhat assuaged my frustration with not having the strength to manage a sailboat on my own. Again, adaptability is the key here. The lesson I share is not to focus on what I cannot do. I consistently ask *What can I do?* I am free to plan variation in each day but usually follow the comfortable variety of activities I've already described.

I missed having the excitement of a man in my life, so I rejoined match.com and again met many. If the telephone interview was satisfactory, we arranged to meet halfway between our two addresses. Sometimes, I would invite the man to my home and other times I would travel to his house, especially when it was conveniently on my way to a farther destination such as a visit to a friend or family. I was not clear what kind of relationship I was looking for, but I was certain I missed the touch, hugs, and kisses of an attractive man. I missed the smell of some men and the hairy arms of others. I did not respond to applicants who were more than ten years my junior.

I made a date with a Columbia University professor to meet on the steps of the New York Public Library next to one of the world-renowned lions. Unfortunately, it poured that day, so we rescheduled to meet at my house. He arrived a few days later by way of the Long Island Railroad and Uber. I welcomed him at my front door and offered him something to drink.

"Do you have any beer?" he asked.

For me, this was a shock. Because of my past history with my ex-husband's drinking, I was wary, and responded by asking "Would you like some freshly made iced tea? I also have orange juice or coffee."

He was even more direct when he asked, "How about a scotch and soda?"

Now in my value system, if I'm looking for a serious relationship, and a stranger is in my house, I do not want to complicate my evaluation with either of us drinking. To be courteous, I considered his efforts to negotiate. Aware of his time and effort to make the difficult trip to my house, I complied with his request for a scotch and soda. I listened to his travel stories and quickly saw a pattern confirming my initial concerns. Each story relayed an adventure set in a bar in a distant country. Within two long hours, I drove him to the train station recognizing my indulgence of some-one I considered *a poor soul.*

Stony Brook University offered courses supported by an Osher Foundation Lifelong Learning grant. I signed up for two courses, one in Politics and Law and the other called History Through Literature. Both were engaging. I rarely missed a class. I watched a man named Joe for sev-eral months, and although I agreed with most of his opin-ions, he frustrated me. He repeatedly raised his hand faster than I did, and the leaders called on him before even ob-serving me.

I decided to meet and possibly charm him, so I moved from the right side and the back of the room to a seat be-hind him on the other side of the room. We talked before class. We talked after class. We talked on the phone. We talked on my deck. Finally, I visited his home and then his bedroom. Later in the week, we were again seated on my deck enjoying the setting sun and the multi-colored summer flowers. As I answered his questions about my work as a psychologist, we appeared to be enjoying the moment. He told me he had been seeing a psychiatrist over several years.

"Are you on medication?" I asked.

"No," he said. "Never needed it."

"Why in the world are you spending time and money on therapy for over three years?" I asked. "You seem to be in pretty good shape. Like all of us, we may have our problems, but this does not make us candidates for counseling."

"I like it," he replied. "The visits are fun. It's another activity to add to my calendar."

He had not asked for an opinion, and perhaps I said too forcefully, "Your psychiatrist is milking you."

He responded, "Medicare is paying for it."

"You really do not seem to really need him." I said.

"I just think of my weekly appointment as if I were meeting with a friend. I agree with you. I no longer have any real issues, but it is fun."

I backed off thinking *Of course, this is business.* We went inside to watch PBS news, and later, we enjoyed another shared meal.

Within days, I realized he was not calling me, so I called him.

"What's happening?" I asked. He said something about no longer being able to see me. Considering that I had thought we were getting emotionally closer, I asked "Why?"

His answer—"We're not a good fit."

"Can you tell me more so I can learn how I misread our friendship?" I asked.

"You're just too much," he said.

Again, I asked "Why?"

"My psychiatrist said so," he replied.

Months later, a librarian friend who danced weekly at the Moose Club said she had met someone there who was perfect for me. She said, "If you do not want to try dancing, watch him playing the bass with a senior group of musicians." This I did and introduced myself. He was a perfect gentleman, courteous, fit, lean, and an excellent escort to many cultural events. However, the chemistry was not there. With care and respect, we stopped dating.

On one trip to DC, I detoured to Palmyra, Virginia, to meet Samuel, a retired optometrist. My hidden agenda was to see more than the photos he had sent me of the estate he had built. He began this passion in his mid-seventies when he and his wife moved from Long Island to Virginia and purchased twenty undeveloped acres of woods. Having the actual property before him, he completed his initial design of the house, hired a contractor, and then actively worked with him and his team in the building of a multi-storied house and environmentally consonant extended gardens.

Now, here I was, arriving ten years after his initial move from Long Island to Virginia. He had been a widower for almost ten years and was looking for a mate. I found him on his knees laying tile in a new addition. His old hound quietly snored next to him. Samuel finished laying the tile he had been working with and stood to greet me, deferring a handshake until he washed. Having quit for the day, he then offered me the one rocking chair in the great room which appeared inconsequential under the soaring cape of the multi-windowed cathedral ceiling. He sat on an old arm chair, and we continued sharing our respective histories and our agendas for these retirement years. He was clearly lonely having had two prior female long-term guests who may have shared his bed. Each had answered his ad arriving with their children. Each created a facsimile of family life, but I saw it as a temporary fantasy.

As we talked, the room was darkening, and I was hungry. I offered to cook a meal, but he had no food in the house and did not know where the frying pan was. He said he could make coffee in the morning, but he wanted to take me to the one restaurant in town, where the staff treated him as family and expected us for supper in the diner.

We returned to his house and he carried my bag to my bedroom. Initially I did not see the magnificence of the floor-to-ceiling stained-glass window in my bathroom, the one he had designed in memory of his wife. However, the next morning, he told me his greatest pleasure was in creating beautiful objects and spaces including two other stained-glass windows, the house, and the environmentally conservative landscaping.

Each of the two women with their children were to be homemakers for him. To me, they sounded like opportunists or thieves. He complained of missing some antique furniture, but he never mentioned the possibility these women had taken advantage of him despite their abrupt, unannounced departures. The next morning, I walked the rough, unadulterated terrain, and I could see how his vision of sustaining the natural environment succeeded. His boardwalks, his redirecting and expanding the creeks, his introduction of native plants into the gardens and the koi ponds reflected his love and respect for nature. An award by the county for "Building consistent with environmental sustainability" hung in the entrance hall.

He was sitting on that hallway's steps with his dog at his feet as I kissed him on the cheek to say a gentle good-bye and said, "Take care." I knew he would never leave this remote, beautiful wilderness, and I knew I would never return. As I drove down the long driveway perfectly lined with pear trees, I felt sad about our mortality, especially those of us with passion.

Returning to the illusion of a predictable life on Long Island, I had a follow-up appointment with my oncologist for the 2005 lymphoma. My labs showed that I was again under attack with a different kind of cancer, this time Peritoneal Ovarian Cancer, Stage IV. This now is a chronic disease effectively limiting my energy for time in the gym, but not joy, excitement, and enthusiasm for new friends and creative activities. I joined another book club and continued on the board of the yacht club.

A trip to Puerto Rico with Bob, my friend of forty-five years, followed my second treatment with chemotherapy. When Bob said he was going to Puerto Rico that evening in late August 2018, I impetuously decided to invite myself along. Beyond the flight and the first night in a hotel he had booked, I had no idea what I was getting into except I knew I had a backup and escort in Bob. I knew little about the aftermath of the two hurricanes that had destroyed the infrastructure of the island.

Since the 1970s, Bob has remained an exciting personality, an intermittent friend with many stories of adventure and surprising travel experiences. His first wife was a Playboy bunny. The second, an Indian he met at a rock concert in New Delhi, and his third, a German teacher of English he had met on a ski train in the Alpines of Italy. He finds it very easy to engage strangers because he has a facility with languages and truly enjoys their stories.

When Gene and I shared meals or traveled with him, I had not recognized that the presence of male friends mellowed his intensity, I wasn't prepared for how difficult it would be to find harmony with just the two of us. When he expected to be in charge of the car rental, I felt cared for, but when he seemed to be dangerously speeding on hairpin turns up and down the mountains, I felt terror. When the edges of the road edges crumbled next to steep downward, rock-strewn inclines, I forcefully yelled at him "Stop the car. Let me sit behind you."

Grumbling, he argued "You're nuts. There is nothing wrong with my driving."

My rejection of his driving style probably established the beginning of our trials. I became extremely anxious. When the hair pin curves became bobby pin turns, always on a one and a half lane road, I really wanted out, but the car was registered only under his insurance. He would not accept my taking the wheel, nor did he modify his speed.

He was a mix of generosity and then complaint. Puerto Rico was in no way adequately prepared for tourists unless they booked a resort and stayed there, using a limousine or taxi to visit other areas. We did not want an orchestrated tour or cosseted accommodations. We intended to travel the entire coastline and sample most of the renowned coastal resort beaches without extravagant costs. This was not realistic as we booked our sleeping quarters day by day. The rooms were often in barrios without street signs or clerks capable of enough English to help us get there.

In addition to a lack of street names in areas which had no or little lights, most inhabitants spoke no English. We were often rescued unexpectedly by individuals connected to New York. Even non English speakers would jump into their car to lead the way to our reserved housing and sometimes accepted a cash gift for their time and fuel. Bob argued that they did not need the money, so I said it was out of my pocket. Later, he became more willing to pay for the extra help but still concluded most of the Puerto Ricans were poor managers and should have recovered from the devastation incurred from the hurricanes. He asked, "How could they not speak English? How could they not have street signs in highly-populated barrios? How could they not have Interstate Highway intersections marked with legible signs? Why were the traffic lights still not working?" We learned to start locating our next sleeping reservation by 4 pm, but that was often of little help because some addresses were hidden behind other housing. One was even on a different island reachable by ferry. We did not go there and found different housing at 11pm through the kindness of a gracious Puerto Rican attorney we met at a petrol station.

The problem was more than Bob having little understanding or feeling for a country that had been knocked flat. He really seemed to be unable to discriminate a second world country from first world cultures. He was prepared for closed roads in El Yungue National Park, but then complained when the national park was not totally open. "How can the Puerto Ricans not have restored access to this major rainforest? I have not been to a rainforest. I expected this one to be open."

Bob also criticized the cost of my iPhone. "Why would you buy something so expensive when an android would do?" When his phone had no internet or working GPS access, he expected me to immediately use apps on my phone that I knew nothing about. "Hurry up. Why can't you find that address right away?" Finally, if he needed me to get a direction from a clerk in a shop, he'd say "Hurry up. Hop out. I'll wait here." At that point, I turned and said "Bob. My hopping days are over. I've told you, but you don't get it. You need to get this into your head. I have cancer. My hopping days are over." And then, in the extreme heat and the tension we were generating, I felt the corners of my eyes tighten. I teared. He finally received that message with a blank look.

We had no difficulties enjoying remarkable food. We also had fun walking through some of the beach towns and contrasting access points to the beaches. Sometimes we followed a littered, filthy path and other times, palms or a board walk that indicated the way. One entrance off the main road had become the home of a dog pack, a bitch and five offspring. They did not approach us. We did not bother them. For me, unexpected closed bridges were part of the game, a challenge to achieve a destination without an accurate map. His chronic grumbling about "what is not", rather than accepting "what is", lead me back to the many self-relaxation techniques I had taught others.

Lots of deep breathing and self-talk kept me calm as I reconsidered an option to make an early departure.

I decided I wanted to complete this journey and intentionally decided to finish the trip with Bob. Our last stop was at an elite resort with three swimming pools, waterside bars, extra large towels and international guests eager for conversation. We self-indulged with no difficulty.

As planned we arrived midday in the states. We parted without words of anger, just a goodbye hug. I do not expect him to check in with me until he needs the support of an old friend. He remains an iridescent, unpredictable butterfly that gives me pleasure and laughter in small doses.

Chapter Eighteen

"I ride the horse. I do not watch the race."

I have greedily lived my eighty years without seriously choosing to take time to write about my thoughts, decisions, or values. In 2017, I survived a different kind of cancer with subsequent and definitely inconvenient complications. In 2018, the ovarian cancer returned. Today, I have less confidence in my physical strength or sustainable energy. This book has fostered an understanding of my evolution as a strong woman.

More than simply understanding and accepting my life choices, I am actually pleased. I know others may judge me and not agree with my belief system, but I see that as their problem, not mine. I understand the evolution of my choices, and I no longer feel I need to justify what may appear as helter-skelter, wasteful, decisions. I now see the consistency in why, each time I achieved the metaphorical equivalent of climbing to the top of the mountain and then choosing to turn from that achievement and choose another way of being. Each time my goal was to intensify my experience, to retain a passion and joy for what is.

I had decided what is important in a life well lived and concluded that not working forever to pay for taxes, large houses, and furniture was one value. Eating well was another. I had wanted the freedom and adventure of life on a sailboat and was willing to live frugally to make this happen. But with aging, this is no longer an option. I am now willing to pay for insurance and taxes and accept the comfort of a house in the woods. Connection to family and friends continues as a priority that is much more accessible. I miss a life partner, but chemistry remains elusive, and this is not a priority.

Recently I realized there is a man, a few years older than my son, whom I have watched for two years. At a university gathering, I impulsively decided to walk up to Adam and initiate a brief hello. Nothing could be lost in this encounter as I would be leaving in ten minutes and only my body language, ensconced in proper campus clothing, communicated my interest. Our verbal communication appeared benign, but my goodbye hugs sent the message. I had clearly leaned toward him, allowing no physical distance. Then I asked for a second hug. This he vigorously provided, and I left the Great Room. A few days later, he contacted me, and we have developed a relationship like no other I have ever experienced. There is no small talk, no deep conversation, no walks on the beach, no signs of recognition should we see each other. Our relationship is based on sexual play when there is a free hour or two or three. I remain amazed how chemistry can override all the traditional courtship guidelines. The day after our first encounter when he walked into my foyer and decisively kissed me, we puddled to the oriental carpet. Afterward, I found myself in a continuing state of euphoria. I sent him a text asking, "What's a woman to do when the scent of a man lingers on her red shirt?" He replied "Ha, ha. You'll manage." I did and within two days, we set up another assignation. Without guilt, I enjoy looking forward to our next sharing of time and bodies. I realize how much I value my creative sexual play without judgment, censorship, or entanglements. "There are no rules" is the basis for what we have discovered about ourselves. Each event during this year is original. Of course neither violence nor pain are ever in the picture. With certainty, I know these moments will end. Meanwhile, I enjoy the moments.

A few months ago, I backed off from further meetings with Adam because I wanted to explore the possibility of an absolutely traditional relationship. I had tapped another individual on the shoulder, and he responded with interest. To honestly explore the traditional, I had to eliminate my time with Adam. This was done without drama. I then dated and had many long conversations with this extremely vulnerable newcomer, a generous, intelligent, ostensibly kind, financially-comfortable widower. After four weeks of "discussing" ad infinitum, I realized our underlying, significant values were not congruent. I began expressing more forcefully what I considered significant relationships and no longer tried to create bonding when I realized this was totally impossible. I knew he could not tolerate a partner, let alone a friend, who did not perceive him as the authority on everything. By the next day, he called to say "I've enjoyed our time together, but I have too many commitments and feel overwhelmed with too many activities. Please understand you're an interesting woman, but I do not have the energy to go further."

I was absolutely relieved that I had played the game so that I did not have to reject him. A month later, I was surprised at my anger with myself for playing the fool and accepting his misplaced self-confidence, his certainty on what he perceives as the good life. He imagined his female partner would echo his values and thoughts and remain essentially invisible to his extensive cadre of followers. He expected her to follow the traditional commitments of marriage without the perks. Of course, if he ever reads this, he will convincingly say my analysis of what I had experienced was delusional. However, I cannot imagine how I allowed myself to follow into that way of thinking which had painfully set me up for my first marriage.

After that phone call from the man who knew everything, I accepted the fact that it was unlikely I could ever thrive in any kind of traditional relationship. I notified Adam that the "traditional possibility" was no longer a possibility for me.

"When you have time, do let me know."

He replied, "My new job keeps me on a tight schedule."

I replied, "Congratulations."

Five minutes later he called back and asked if I were available two days hence.

As we again met in my foyer, he asked, "How are you with time on the deck?"

I said, "Brilliant idea."

We quickly grabbed white quilts and one pillow, trusting the early morning temperature and gentle breeze to be perfect as we settled under the canopy of hardwoods trees and inhaled the scent of the colorful deck flowers. We spoke briefly about my plans for chemo. We shared, with unusual honesty, the unavoidable reality of the challenges in living. The spontaneity, setting, and activity with Adam created another absolutely new experience, which left me smiling, especially during yoga the next day. I worked really hard to strengthen those exotic positions I know my partner will appreciate.

My energy, considered notable by others, derives from an attitude to feed my insignificant organism with the best possible fuel possible, and to internalize deeply the joy of each moment. I regret sometimes making what I thought were informed, thought out, caring decisions which harmed myself or others. These were active behaviors, chosen risks. And as I stated at the beginning of this chapter, I am not passive. I do not watch the race. I ride the horse. I do not spend my time endlessly worrying about the "What if's." Of this I am proud. Given the outlines of my life, the warp, I admit I continue to choose new directions in my script, much like the weaver's choice of the pattern of the weft.

As soon as we start breathing and being, we begin dying. Between the two, we have the potential for great adventure and great discoveries—about ourselves and about this world we occupy for such a short time. Benjamin Disraeli said, "Life is too short to be little." I say we can live fully wherever we are and whatever our circumstances. In the far or not-so-far future, when I lie dying, I imagine I will think: Oh, this is a new experience. I wonder what will be beyond *this* mountain.

ABOUT THE AUTHOR

Integrating psychology, philosophy, and experience, Anita Vlismas, Ph.D., shares methods and attitudes on how to live with and reframe pain, how to become a creator rather than a consumer, and how to choose without fear.

A natural story teller, Vlismas had been advised since age twenty to write. Instead, she purposefully chose to live her life with intention and focus. Although many women in the seventies were changing their expectations of life, the author's palette provided extreme options rarely considered by her peers.

Now eighty years old, she describes how she began. With minimal financial resources or family support, she has lived her life with thoughtfulness, persistence, and the capacity to question every rule, script, expectation, and theology. She reminds us we are individuals in all senses of the word and yet, paradoxically, we are also, inexorably, part of "The All", the undeniable eternity.

50143167R00138

Made in the USA
Columbia, SC
03 February 2019